D1634034

REMINISCENCES OF DOLLAR
& TILLICOULTRY

DOLLAR,

FROM THE SOUTH BRIDGE.

Published by T. Bradshaw, Bookseller.

Eng. by Banks & Co.

Edinburgh

REMINISCENCES

OF

DOLLAR, TILLICOULTRY,

AND OTHER DISTRICTS ADJOINING THE OCHILS,

WITH

Notes on Progress, Scientific Discovery, and Invention of New Spinning Machinery, during the last Hundred Years.

By WILLIAM GIBSON,

TILLICOULTRY,

Second Edition.

STRONG OAK PRESS

This Edition © Spa Books & The Strong Oak Press 1990

All rights reserved. No part of this publication may be
reproduced, stored in a retrieval system or transmitted
in any form, by any means electrical or mechanical or
otherwise without first seeking the written permission
of the copyright owner and of the publisher.

ISBN: 1-871048-18-4

Publishing History: This work was first issued in 1882,
a second edition followed in 1883. It is the second edition
which is reproduced here, complete and unabridged.

Published by The Strong Oak Press
          Spa Books Ltd
          PO box 47
          Stevenage
          Herts SG2 8UH

Printed in Great Britain by
Antony Rowe Ltd, Chippenham, Wiltshire

PREFATORY NOTE TO THE FIRST EDITION.

—o—

WHEN I commenced to take these notes I thought they might extend to a dozen or two pages, and intended to have only one manuscript copy; but finding, as I progressed, that this number was going to be largely exceeded, it then occurred to me that I would have them printed, for private circulation amongst my friends, or others who may feel interested in seeing them.

W. G.

TILLICOULTRY, *July* 1, 1882.

PREFATORY NOTE TO THE SECOND EDITION.

——o——

THE First Edition of this book was printed for private circulation, but a very general wish having been expressed that it should be made public, I have now carried this into effect, by preparing this Second Edition. With the exception of some slight alterations and additions, the narrative continues throughout the same as before, *and as written in* 1882. The additions are numerous, and some of them of considerable length, and may, I hope, give additional interest to the book.

W. G.

TILLICOULTRY, *December* 1, 1883.

CONTENTS.

CHAPTER I.

CHAPTER II.

CHAPTER III.

CHAPTER IX.

CHAPTER X.

LIST OF ILLUSTRATIONS.

——o——

PLATES.

WOODCUTS.

REMINISCENCES.

CHAPTER I.

BLACKFORD: ITS OLD CHURCH AND CHURCHYARD.

THE ruined walls of the old Parish Church of Blackford, and old burying-ground, are beautifully situated
on the top of a high knoll to the north-east of the
village, and immediately above the railway station.
From it can be obtained a fine view of the surrounding
country, including a long stretch of the beautiful Ochil
Hills to the south. Below it lies the quiet village of
Blackford, built not in the usual irregular fashion
throughout Scotland, but in two regular parallel streets,
from end to end of the village, with a number of short
regular streets or lanes running at right angles between
the two. The south street is the old town of Blackford,
and forms part of the old highway from Perth to Stirling. It was along it that, on Saturday the 12th day
of November 1715 (167 years ago), the Earl of Mar,
with his army of Highlanders, marched from Auchterarder to meet the Duke of Argyle, with some 5000
royal troops, in the neighbourhood of Dunblane, and

A

on the following day fought the stubborn battle of Sheriffmuir.

Mar left Perth on Thursday the 10th of November, and reached the battlefield on Saturday night; and on Sabbath the 13th November, about noon, the battle commenced, and raged so long and furiously that darkness alone put an end to it. At the close of the day it was hard to tell which side had gained the victory, which gave rise to the following amusing lines :—

> ' Some say that we wan,
> Some say that they wan,
> And some say that nane wan at a', man ;
> But o' ae thing I'm sure,
> That at Sheriffmuir
> A battle there was that I saw, man.'

I may in passing refer to what led to this famous battle of Scottish history.

On the death of Queen Anne in 1714, George, Elector of Hanover, succeeded to the British crown ; but a great portion of the inhabitants of Scotland (notably the Highland clans) had wished James Francis Edward, commonly called 'The Chevalier,' instead, and, headed by the Earl of Mar, determined to raise the standard of revolt, and get this foreigner deposed and their favourite put in his place. Hence the rebellion of 1715.

Some idea may be formed of the feeling in Scotland regarding George I. from the following couplet :—

> ' Wha the deil ha'e we gotten for a king
> But a wee, wee German lairdie.'

A good many of the houses in this south street of Blackford are very old, but it has also some good new buildings ; while the north street—which is the more modern part of the village—has some fine new houses, with two beautiful churches, the Established and the Free, with handsome spires and clocks, which give the village quite a smart appearance.

One of the principal industries of the village is brewing, for which it has long been celebrated—Blackford ales being well known throughout Scotland. There are three pretty large breweries, only two of which are at present in operation; but although they must carry on pretty extensive businesses, they do not, unfortunately, give employment to many hands.

About a dozen of hand-loom weavers, or so, still get occasional employment from Auchterarder; but as a weaving village, its day has gone by.

Before the introduction of the power-loom, however, Blackford, like many villages in Scotland, used to get a weekly supply of webs from Glasgow, which were sent to agents who gave out the webs to the weavers, superintended the weaving, and got the cloth returned to the city; and thus employment was given to very many hands. But this is all changed now. The introduction of steam and the power-loom have concentrated very much the manufacturing of all these goods in the large cities, where large public power-loom factories have been built, the proprietors of which weave goods to any one; and very extensive manufacturing firms in Glasgow get all their weaving done there, and are not possessed of a single loom themselves, except for making patterns on. The proprietors of these establishments are called 'job weavers,' and some of them are possessed of very large premises, with many hundreds of looms, do a large trade, and are possessed of considerable wealth. Cloth can be woven in these factories at a mere tithe of what it used to cost on the old hand-loom; and hence these small weaving villages throughout Scotland have been ruined, so far as weaving is concerned.

Another flourishing industry that was at one time carried on very extensively in Blackford, and gave employment to a great many hands, has now dwindled down to very small dimensions, and must have told greatly on the prosperity and stir of the village; and that was the tanning and currying of leather, and the manufacture of boots and shoes for the wholesale trade of the country. Although still carried on to a moderate extent, few hands, comparatively, are now employed, for the bulk of this trade is now concentrated in steam factories throughout the country, where, with the aid of the sewing-machine, shoes can be produced at a price that hand-made goods have no chance with; and hence this industry, like the hand-loom weaving, has suffered greatly in Blackford. From these two causes it is now a very quiet village, and the first time I paid a visit to it—in March of this year—I was struck with the great silence that reigned throughout it, and thought it a very rural village indeed. Though quiet in the village, there is plenty of noise adjoining it, however; for throughout the day, and night also, the 'iron horse' on the Caledonian Railway (which passes close to the village) snorts away almost constantly, the number of trains during the twenty-four hours on this great iron road to the north of Scotland being very great indeed.

The beautiful water of the Allan passes close to the village, and is (even so near the top of Strathallan) of considerable size, and is considered a very fine trout-fishing stream. Danny Burn, from the Ochils, which passes close to the west side of the village, joins the Allan a little below it. The foot-road through the Ochils, by Backhill House and the Devon to Tillicoultry and Dollar, goes up by Kinpauch House, and before the introduction of the railway was largely used by pedestrians between the north and south sides of the Ochils.

I have been thus particular in giving a description of Blackford, from the fact that it was the birthplace of the writer's grandfather, of whom I will speak more particularly farther on in this narrative.

From a tablet on the inside of the north wall of the old church, we learn that the good people of Blackford had been long honoured in having a baronet for their minister, one of the ancestors of the present Sir Henry Wellwood Moncreiff, Bart., of Tullibole, Fossoway. The inscription runs thus :—

THE REVEREND SIR WILLIAM MONCREIFF, BART.,

MINR. BLACKFD., ORDAINED 1738.

DIED 9TH DECR. 1767, AGED 61.

AND

MRS. KATHERINE WELLWOOD, HIS WIFE,

WHO DIED 31ST MARCH 1768, AGED 45 YEARS.

My purpose, however, in drawing attention to this old church and churchyard of Blackford is more especially to take notice of a very interesting tombstone (so far as the writer's relatives are concerned) lying flat on the ground about the centre of the churchyard, and which, from the date on it (1739), must have been placed there a year after Sir William Moncreiff, Bart., was ordained to the parish. I herewith give a rough sketch of this stone, with that part of the inscription which is plainly readable, the rest of it, unfortunately, being too much wasted to make clearly out what it is, although words are still traceable.

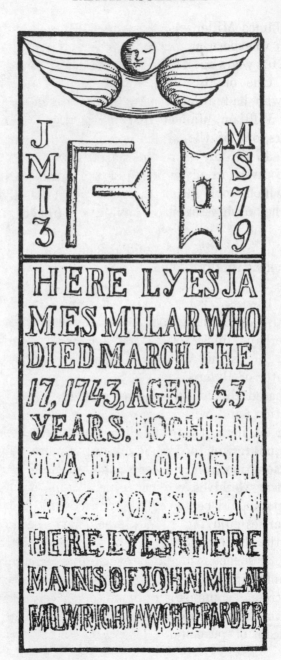

The James Miller who was buried beneath this stone, and who was born at the Mill of Duchally in the year 1680 (202 years ago), was the writer's great-great-grandfather. One of this James Miller's sons was named James, who had a family of nine children—four sons (named William, James, John, and David) and five daughters, one of the latter of whom was named Jean, born in 1746, my grandmother by my father's side, and who lived in my father's house in Dollar till her death, which took place in October 1842, she being then in her ninety-seventh year.

KINCARDINE GLEN, DUCHALLY MILL, AND AUCHTERARDER.

The Mill of Duchally is in one of the most picturesque glens, perhaps, in Scotland—the beautiful water of the Ruthven (or, as the Auchterarder folks generally call it, ' the Water of Riven ') flowing through the centre of it. It is situated directly south from Crieff Junction railway station, and within ten minutes' walk of it; but although so near, this really beautiful glen is almost entirely unknown to the many thousands who daily pass that station. If its beauties were known, I have no doubt it would have very many visitors, for no more lovely spot could be selected for a day's outing, and for picnic parties enjoying themselves. This deep gorge or glen of the Ruthven, of some 150 feet deep, and from 700 to 800 feet wide at the top (called Kincardine Glen from Kincardine Castle, the old seat of the Duke of Montrose), commences at the north end of Gleneagles, and runs nearly due east, with the beautiful little stream of pure water running at the bottom of it, which empties itself into the Earn some dozen of miles away.

For a good distance above the mill, and about half a mile below it, the steep sloping banks are beautifully green, with here and there clumps of fine old trees, forming quite a romantic scene, and just such a place as one would like to shut himself in for a day from the bustling outside world. About half a mile below the mill, the fine policies around Kincardine Castle commence, and the glen is densely wooded down to the water's edge, and is really one of the most romantic spots one could wish to see.

On the high ground not far from the mill, the farm-house of The Barns is situated, and here it was that the Duke of Montrose, when resident in Kincardine Castle, kept his retainers; and many a struggle would no doubt take place between them and the Duke of Argyle's clansmen residing at Castle Campbell (romantically situated in the beautiful glen above Dollar)—a deadly feud having long existed between the two houses. The distance between the two strongholds would not be more than a dozen of miles or so, and two roads were available, one through Gleneagles, and the other by the Borland Glen. The old road through Gleneagles is still distinctly traceable, near the bottom of the glen, and on the opposite side from the present road.

The Miller family of Duchally Mill and Auchterarder, at the beginning of the eighteenth century, carried on the trade of wheelwrights, that of making spinning-wheels for the young brides of those days, for no young wife thought of taking up house without that most essential piece of furniture, and the making of them was a trade by itself. At that time the spinning of yarn was all done by hand, and the wool carded with hand cards;

and thus almost every household carded and spun their own yarn, and gave it to weavers to weave into cloth, for the clothing of their households. Then it was that ' homespun ' cloths were a reality, and not, as now-a-days, a name given to a cloth which our manufacturers make in imitation of them.

What a contrast to all this now exists at the present day! The introduction of the carding engine, and the invention of the spinning mule, have completely revolutionized this old state of matters; and now can be seen in any of our large factories as many as from 30,000 to 40,000 spindles, spinning yarn, and each spindle turning off as much as at least five women could do with the old hand spinning-wheel; thus the production of one mill is now as great as that of 150,000 to 200,000 hand wheels.

The making of spinning-wheels by the Millers of Auchterarder gradually developed into a general wright's and cabinet-making trade, which has been carried on very extensively and successfully up till the present time. Mr. David Miller* (who retired from the business some time ago) is a great-grandson of the James Miller who was born in 1680, and Mrs. Tainsh (who is nearly ninety years of age) is a great-grand-daughter.

The principal occupation of the inhabitants of Auchterarder in my young days was hand-loom weaving, the webs being supplied (as in Blackford) from Glasgow. Now there are three large factories in the town, which supply webs to those who still continue at the hand-loom, while they give employment to a very large number of women at the power-loom, of which there will be well on for a thousand.

---

* Regarding Mr. Miller and some others referred to in the following pages, see Appendix to the First Edition.

Fifty years ago, Auchterarder was very poorly supplied with water, and in dry seasons it had to be carted, in barrels, up from the 'Water of Riven.' They have now, however, got an abundant supply of fine, pure water, from beyond the Muir of Auchterarder; and for this the town was very much indebted to the exertions, along with others, of Mr. David Miller, who took an active part in getting it introduced, which was done in 1832.

In order to get information about my progenitors, Mr. Miller and I paid a visit to Blackford Churchyard in the month of March of this year; and, after about an hour's work, in 'Old Mortality' style, succeeded in laying bare the inscription on the old family tombstone, which turned out to be of such very great interest to us both. It was covered with green mould of about half an inch thick.

DOLLAR——RELATIVES——CASTLE CAMPBELL.

My grandfather, James Gibson, was born in Blackford in 1756; and married Jean Miller of Auchterarder in 1780 or 1781.

As grandfather died in 1819, before I was born, I am indebted for any information regarding him to my elder relatives. He was a tall, stout man, with reddish hair; very pushing and enterprising; of an affable and genial disposition, and was a general favourite with the good folks of Dollar.

Grandmother (who died in 1842) I remember well, as she lived in my father's house till her death. She had been a most active woman in her day, and to her energy and business tact their success in after life was not a little indebted.

They commenced business in two small houses in the old town of Dollar, in the north street that leads up to Castle Campbell, where Mr. Miller's hall (at present a grain store) was afterwards built.

Like most country shops in those days, they dealt in almost everything—groceries, drapery goods, hardwares, etc.; and, from a very small beginning, their business gradually extended, and became the principal emporium, for almost everything, for the district for miles around. With what success they prosecuted their calling may be judged of from the fact that, in 1806, grandfather built the large dwelling-house and shop farther down the village, at present occupied by Mr. Hunter, and where, for forty years, the business was successfully carried on—first by grandfather, and then by my father, and where the writer, and the rest of the family, were born and brought up.

In those early days, and before the introduction of spinning machinery, business was very differently conducted from what it is now, and Mrs. Tainsh has told me that she remembers well of grandfather coming north to Monzie ('Monee') market, to buy blankets and plaidings, and calling at Auchterarder on his way there.

The yarn was spun by the women of the parish, and also in the Highlands beyond, on their spinning wheels; woven into blankets and plaidings, and sold in the annual market held at Monzie. As a fair specimen of how goods were manufactured in those early days, and of one of our rural weaving villages at that time, I may here introduce the account given of Monzie parish in the statistical account of Scotland, in regard to its manufactures, written by the Rev. George Erskine, in the year 1792. He says :—'The principal industry in the parish is that of weaving. They weave all kinds of plain and tweeled linen, and woollen cloth ; and these not only for their own use, but also for sale ; the chief kinds of cloth made by them are plaiden, linen, and scrims. The plaiden they sell at from 10d. to 14d. per yard. They make a very large quantity of linen cloth, and bleach it excellently themselves ; it is of various degrees of fineness, and they sell it at from 1s. to 4s. per yard. Some families, where there are only two looms, have made and sold 1000 yards per annum. The scrim is a narrow linen cloth, of different degrees of fineness, and which they sell without bleaching it. It is all exported, perhaps for trousers. The women spin a great deal of yarn, which they make into cloth for sale, and thus by their industry raise a part of their rent. . . . Number of weavers in the parish, 54. . . . There is only one yearly market in the parish, when every house, hut, and shade is converted into a dram-shop ;—it is held in the middle of August.'

When spinning machinery was afterwards introduced, plaidings and blankets were manufactured in Tillicoultry and Alva, and the market for them was changed to Perth ; and thither the manufacturers of our neighbourhood used to go regularly to dispose of their wares. This market must have been discontinued about the year 1840 ; for, after that time, the manufactures of our district were sold to wholesale houses in the large cities, principally in Glasgow. When I came to Tillicoultry in 1847, I used to hear many stories about our manufacturers attending Perth market.

Grandfather had two sisters and a brother—Margaret and Emily ; but his brother's name I have not been able to find out, nor have I been able to trace clearly what became of him, further than that he settled somewhere in England, was married, and had a family, and that two of his daughters once paid a visit to my late married sister in Stirling, Mrs. Dalgleish, which must have been more than forty-three years ago, as she died in 1839. Margaret married a Mr. Ritchie, and I can learn of only two of her family—Mr. William Ritchie of Portobello (I am not aware whether he still survives or not), and the late Mrs. Whitehead of Perth. Emily married a Mr. John Lawson of Blackford, who commenced business as a brewer in Glendevon, and died there, leaving his widow with a large family. After the death of her husband, grandfather brought his widowed sister and her family to Dollar, where they afterwards resided in one of his houses, nearly opposite his own. Her descendants are very numerous at the foot of the Ochils at the present day—Mr. Edward Moir, Tillicoultry (at present eighty-three years of age), being a grandson; whilst her great-grandchildren and great-great-grandchildren are very numerous. Mr. Lawson draper, Alloa, is a great-grandson.

Grandfather's family consisted of three—two sons and a daughter, named William, James, and Janet, the last of whom died in infancy. Whether my father or Uncle James was eldest, I have not been able to find out; but, from the record in my father's family Bible, Uncle James died on the first Sabbath of July 1812, when quite a young man.

I was not aware, till the other day, that I am really descended from a wool-spinner (the business I have now been engaged in for thirty-five years), but an old and respected native of Dollar informs me that Grandfather Gibson, a Robert Pitcairn, and John Burns (father of the first Mrs. Peter Stalker—Eliza Burns) formed themselves into a company, and built the first wool mill in Dollar; and that one Willie Wilson was the manager. This mill was situated between the upper bridge and Mrs. Bell's Hall (formerly the second wool mill), and stood parallel to the burn; and the water for the wheel of it was brought in a lade from the weir (now entirely demolished) at the public bleaching-green, down past the foot of the gardens, where the Castle Walk is now formed. This original mill was entirely removed when the second mill was built, some sixty years ago. Like most country mills at that time, it was for carding and spinning country wool, and the yarn was made into goods—blankets, plaidings, cloths, etc.— by weavers throughout the village, for the use of the respective parties who sent in the wool; and thus, in a sense, each family was its own manufacturer. This practice is still continued in many country places, and especially in the Highlands, at the present day, where many thriving country mills are still carried on.

To show the price of wool at that period, I have learned, on undoubted authority, that Mr. John Burns bought a Glendevon clip of black-faced wool, one year, at the very low price of 5s. 6d. per stone (2¾d. per lb.).

Mr. Burns was, by the way, like very many in those days, a famous fiddler, and his services were had in great request on festive occasions.

Having referred to the public bleaching-green, I may here give a short account of how it was acquired by the people of Dollar.

In the end of last century a petition was got up for presentation to the then Lord of the Manor—the Duke of Argyle—to grant a piece of ground for a public bleaching-green, and Mr. William M'Leish (the Rev.

John M'Leish's father) was despatched to Inveraray Castle, to present it to his Grace. After the long and tedious journey was accomplished, and the castle reached at last, Mr. M'Leish was ushered into the presence of the butler—a thorough-bred, true-born Highlandman, and one who would have fought to the last drop of his blood to uphold the dignity of the house of the great M'Callum-Mohr. After the usual civilities had passed between this dignitary and William, something like the following conversation took place, which the latter ever afterwards used to tell with the greatest gusto.

WILLIAM (on seeing a pony-phaeton driving in through the Castle grounds, with a gentleman, dressed in tartan, in it). ' What gentleman will that be ?'

DUGALT. 'That, sir, iss a nopleman ; that pe his Grace ta Tuke of Argyle, ant faar apove eny mere shentlemans.'

W. ' But you are surely joking ; the great Duke would never drive in a small phaeton like that !'

D. 'No, sir, I am not joking ; and that iss shust ta Tuke. He hafe thirteen graant carriages, but he shooses to trive in ta wan that you see him in, ant we have no pusiness.'

W. ' But surely he must have few horses when he drives with a little beastie like that ?'

D. ' Few horses ! Dit you'l only saw his thirty graant horses, you neffer see ta like ov them pefore, nor neffer will to again, neffer.'

W. ' But surely my Lord would never dress with a common tartan kilt like that gentleman ?'

D. ' You are not to call him " My Lort," for a Tuke iss faar apove a Lort ; ant as for his tress, it iss his Grace's pleasure to wear ta kilt ; but he hafe neffer so many peautiful tress, as you neffer see pefore, neffer.'

W. 'Well, well, I must not doubt your word any longer, but believe that it *was really* the Duke I saw; and now I would like to see his Grace, and present the petition I have come with from the inhabitants of Dollar.'

D. 'Yiss, yiss, I will now take you to ta Tuke's shamber, but rememper you are not to say, " from ta inhapitants of Tollar," but " from ta Lordship of Campbell;" ant when you leafe ta Tuke's presence, you must walk packwards, shust ta same as from ta King's presence.'

Mr. M'Leish was kindly entertained by order of the Duke; and the result of the interview was that the petition was favourably received; and in a few weeks word came to Dollar that a free grant, in perpetuity, was given of the piece of ground petitioned for. The entrance to this bleaching-green is by the back of the houses on the north side of ' Hillie's Close.'

When referring to Inveraray Castle, I think it may not be out of place here, to give a thoroughly characteristic specimen of the genuine *'Hielan'* proclamations that the good folks of the county-town of Inveraray were at one time called on to listen to. With stentorian lungs, Donalt, the town-crier, was heard one day making known the following terrible warning through the streets of the town :—

'T—Ahoy, ant T—Ahoy again, ant ta—hither Ahoy—three times ! ! !   Whisht ! ! !

'If eny person or persons iss caugcht fushin' apoon ta Loch, or under ta Loch, or through ta Loch, or in ta Loch, she shall pe persecute with three persecutions.   First, she shall pe droont, then she shall pe purnt, and syne she shall pe hangit.   Ant if she'll evermore come pack again to do ta same thing, she shall pe veesit with a faar waur death.

'God pless ta Tuke ov Argyle.'

We should think there would not be much fishing of any kind round Inveraray for many a long day after this.

Behind the second wool mill (which is the only one I remember of) there was a large, deep pond, for running the dirty Waulk Mill water into; and this was emptied occasionally during the night, and the burn not polluted when people were requiring water. It was a most dangerous place for children, although I don't recollect of any one ever being drowned in it, but many a poor kitten ended its days there. This mill pond was in the next garden to my father's, and was a well-known place to us all.

The inhabitants of Dollar were, I believe, indebted to the Rev. Dr. Mylne for the construction of this pond, and the preserving to them of their beautiful stream of pure water. Previous to his coming to Dollar, the dirty Waulk Mill water had been regularly run into the burn, and greatly polluted it; and against this nuisance the doctor sent a strongly-worded protest to the manager of the mill, and insisted on its being stopped at once. Not knowing the calibre of the man he had to deal with, Willie Wilson sent him back a joking answer, telling him he didn't see the need of making such an ado about it, and 'that the water would make fine cream to his tea.' However, he soon found out he had mistaken his man, and that the doctor was in earnest, and not to be trifled with, and that some plan must be adopted at once to allay the wrath of the new priest. Accordingly, the big pond was devised, and carried into execution; and thus the nuisance was put an end to.

My father had decided to join grandfather in the now thriving business of general merchants, and after grandfather's death carried on the business successfully for

B

twenty-seven years. The shop, during my father's life-time and for long afterwards, was where the parlour of the house now is. It was an emporium for almost everything, and people came from many miles around to it, from Glendevon, Muckart, Crook-of-Devon, Powmill, Blairingone, Forrestmill, etc.

In the course of his business my father paid an annual visit to the farmers of the Ochils, and amongst others with whom he dealt I may mention one or two of the names—Mrs. Low, of the Borland Glen; Mr. Guild, of Glenquhey; Mr. David Taylor, of the Eind, above Auchterarder, etc.

For ironmongery goods, such as grates, fenders, etc., he went always to headquarters,—Carron and Falkirk Ironworks,—and bought at first hand. I remember well of going with him on one of these visits, when a very little boy; and as there were no railways in those days, the journey had to be done on foot. It was a very hot day, and when trudging through the moss between South Alloa and Carron, we couldn't get a drop of drinkable water, and I was almost on the point of giving in. How much the present generation ought to prize the facilities they have for travelling now-a-days; only those who remember those early times can fully appreciate the immense advantages we now enjoy.

Dollar is beautifully situated at the foot of the Ochils, immediately below the ruins of the famous old stronghold of the Duke of Argyle—Castle Campbell; and although a small town, is of very ancient date, John Knox having dispensed the sacrament at Castle Campbell, while the guest of Archibald, fourth Earl of Argyle, in the year 1556; and Thomas Forrest, vicar of Dollar, being a well-known character in Scottish history. The bridge over the Devon, about a mile east

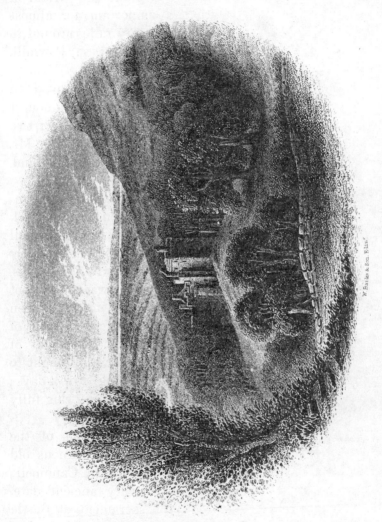

CASTLE CAMPBELL.

W. Banks & Son, Edinr.

from Dollar, where he crossed the stream on his pere-
grinations between the monastery at Inchcolm and
Dollar, still takes its name from him—The Vicar's
Bridge. The following inscription is on it, and was
put there by the well-known antiquarian, the late John
Coventry, Esq. of Devonshaw :—

> Sacred to the memory of THOMAS FORREST, the worthy Vicar
> of Dollar, who among other acts of benevolence built this
> bridge. He died a martyr, A.D. 1538.

This inscription, however, is a little misleading, as the
actual bridge built by the vicar forms only the eastern
half of the arch. It was a narrow bridge, without
ledges, for foot passengers only ; and about eighty years
ago another arch was built alongside the old one, thus
widening the bridge, and making it suitable for conveyances. Low parapet walls were then built, but not
proving sufficient to prevent accidents, the present
higher ones were afterwards substituted.

Authentic records in connection with Castle Campbell date even about a hundred years before John
Knox's time, the oldest title-deeds known for it and the
lands of Dollar being dated the 19th of April 1465—
four hundred and seventeen years ago. They were then
the property of John Stewart, third Lord Innermeath,
and passed into the possession of the Argyle family in
1481, when Colin, first Earl of Argyle, married Isabel
Stewart, one of Lord Innermeath's daughters, and must
have got them along with his bride as a marriage
dowry. The Castle at this time went by the name
of Castle Glaume (Gloom); but in 1489 an Act
of Parliament of James III. was passed, changing it
to Castle Campbell, which would seem to show that
the Argyle family had decided to make it one of their

principal places of residence. How long before 1465
the Castle was built, there is no authentic record, but
it is more than probable it was two or three hundred
years. It continued in the possession of the Argyle
family till 1805 (three and a quarter centuries), when
it was sold to Craufurd Tait, Esq. of Harviestoun, and
is now the property of James Orr, Esq.

Harviestoun and Castle Campbell estates were for a
great many years in the possession of the Globe Insurance Company, but were bought by Sir Andrew Orr in
the year 1859.   Sir Andrew also bought Aberdona
estate in 1860, and that of Sheardale in 1861.   Mr.
Gibson, Dollar—the writer's brother—was appointed
his factor in 1862, and continued to hold the appointment till he resigned in favour of his son, Mr. John. Mr.
James Orr, who succeeded to the estates on the death
of his brother in 1874, is now one of the largest
landed proprietors in the county of Clackmannan.

Castle Campbell was burned in 1644 by the Macleans (who formed part of the Marquis of Montrose's
army) when passing along the valley after the battles of
Auldearn and Alford, and immediately before the battle
of Kilsyth.   And not only was the Castle destroyed, but
all the houses in Dollar and Muckart, with the exception of one in each place (which were saved through a
mistake), the inhabitants of both parishes being vassals
of Argyle.

The Castle is most romantically situated in Dollar
Glen, on a high rocky promontory between the two
burns of Sorrow and Care (or, as they are now called,
the Bank and Turnpike burns), and immediately above
the junction of the two, and is so surrounded by the
deep, densely-wooded, rocky gorges, at the bottom of
which the burns run, that no grander scenery is to be

found, I believe, in Scotland. That this is the general opinion throughout the country is fully borne out by the many thousands who annually visit it, it being evidently considered one of those romantic sights which must not be overlooked. The old tower of the Castle, with its walls of some seven or eight feet thick, shows what a place of great strength it must have been, and before the introduction of artillery must have been almost impregnable. Tradition says that Argyle's retainers were away on a foray of their own when the Macleans attacked and destroyed it, and this seems more than probable, as a very small number of defenders might, in such a situation and with such a stronghold, have defied the whole of the Marquis's army.

In my young days, and for long after, the road to Castle Campbell was by the old cart-road to the north side of the Ochils, that goes up past the Brewlands (so long the abode of Mr. Alexander Stewart), and through Glenquhey. At Gloomhill Quarry a foot-road branched off, down to the bottom of the beautifully-wooded glen; and, after crossing the Turnpike Burn, the ascent to the Castle was made up the almost perpendicular brae, by a series of steps worn out of the turf by the tramp of many hundreds of years. There is now, however, a romantic walk up to the Castle, through the beautiful glen, the whole way; and for this the inhabitants of Dollar are indebted, I believe, to the late Dr. Strachan and Mr. Peter Stalker, who first talked the matter over, and inspected the ground, with the view of making it, and the inhabitants afterwards deserve great credit for the spirited way in which their efforts were seconded; for, by subscriptions, concerts, etc., the handsome sum of £300 was raised to carry the project out. How well this was done must be attested by every one who visits the Castle, for every advantage has been taken of the romantic glen in the formation of the road, and the view from various parts of it is very fine indeed. To stand on the end of the long bridge, at the foot of Kemp's Score, and look around, presents a view that is unsurpassed for grandeur, I believe, anywhere in Britain. The fine scenery, also, at Sochie—above the Castle— was opened up to the visitor by the formation of this walk, which was carried as far up as Nellie's Dell, *b*eyond the fine waterfalls of Upper and Lower Sochie. Until it was formed, few people in Dollar, I believe, had ever seen these beautiful waterfalls, or the deep rocky gorge through which the water for a considerable distance runs.

The first meeting in connection with this walk was held in the Castle Campbell Hotel on the 9th of August 1864—the late Dr. Strachan in the chair— when the following committee was appointed to arrange for a public meeting:—Mr. Stalker, Dr. Strachan, Mr. Bradshaw, Dr. Lindsay, Mr. Brown, Mr. Cousin; Mr. Bradshaw, convener.

On the 15th of August 1864, a public meeting was held, when the following committee was appointed to see to the proper laying out and constructing of the new path:—Mr. Stalker, Dr. Strachan, Mr. Bradshaw, Dr. Lindsay, Mr. Brown, Mr. Cousin, Mr. Westwood, Mr. Horn, Mr. Alexander Wardlaw. Mr. Bradshaw was appointed secretary, and Mr. Wardlaw treasurer.

The public of Dollar are greatly indebted to this committee, and to those who were afterwards added to it, for the great amount of trouble entailed upon them, and the complete success which crowned their labours. Mr. Westwood, Mr. Stalker, and Mr. Horn were of great service to the committee in the engineering part

Banks & Co. Edinr

THE PASS, AND KEMP'S SCORE,
DOLLAR GLEN.

Published by T. Bradshaw, Dollar.

of the work; and Mr. Bradshaw as secretary, and Mr. Wardlaw as treasurer, deserve special thanks for the extra share of work that fell to their lot. Dr. Strachan took a keen interest in the carrying out of the scheme, and for a considerable number of years, and so long as he was able to officiate, acted as chairman at all the meetings held in connection with it.

The footpath was formally opened on the 26th of May 1865, when nearly a thousand people assembled on the ground. At the conclusion of the ceremony, the Dollar Flute Band, which had been in attendance, proceeded through the streets of the village, and played a number of favourite airs.

The open-air proceedings were followed by a supper in the Castle Campbell Hotel—Dr. Strachan in the chair, Mr. Brown and Mr. Westwood acting as croupiers —when eighty gentlemen sat down to supper. The evening was spent very pleasantly, and amongst many other toasts, that of the Lord of the Manor, Sir Andrew Orr, and of Mr. James Cairns, tenant of Dollarbank, were specially proposed, and a vote of thanks tendered to them, for kindly giving their consent to the making of the footpath through the Castle grounds, and those adjoining them.

From a most interesting speech by Mr. James Christie about Castle Campbell, I here give the following short extract:—

'Solitude reigns around, broken only by the dashing cascade, the caw of the rook, or the merry laugh of some visiting party.

> ' The jackdaw nestles in its towers,
> Devoid of every fear,
> And spiders spin their airy webs,
> Where hung the sword and spear.

> ' The warder's tread no more is heard,
>   In echoes deep and long;
>   And in its wild, dismantled ha'
>   Is hushed the minstrel's song.'

During the course of the evening it was announced from the chair that, in honour of the occasion, a new song had been composed by Mr. James Christie, and that it would now be sung by Mr. Deany. It is as follows :—

> ' Winsome lassie, will ye go, will ye go, will ye go?
>   Winsome lassie, will ye go, to the woods o' Castle Campbell?

> ' The Ochils smile in summer dress,
>   The birk-tree waves her silken tress,
>   While nature bathes in loveliness
>   The woodland paths o' Campbell.
>   Winsome lassie, etc.

> ' The burnie dashes doon the glen,
>   O'er rocky scaur, where brackens ben',
>   Or wimples saft by fairy den
>   Among the woods o' Campbell.
>   Winsome lassie, etc.

> ' Sweet scenes o' beauty wait the e'e,
>   Of rifted rock, and flower, and tree,
>   A richer picture couldna be—
>   The leafy glens o' Campbell.
>   Winsome lassie, etc.

> ' We'll roam the Castle's ruined towers,
>   In gloamin's calm and dewy hours,
>   When starnies blink frae siller bowers
>   Upon the woods o' Campbell.
>   Winsome lassie, etc.

> ' Let ithers seek for golden gain
>   On stormy sea or burning plain,
>   Content I'll be wi' you—my ain,
>   Among the woods o' Campbell.
>   Winsome lassie,' etc.

Although the new path was now formally opened. the labours of the committee did not then by any means

Banks & C° Edin.

CRAGINNIN FALL—CASTLE CAMPBELL, N.E.

Published by T Bradshaw, Bookseller Dollar

terminate, but went on for the long period of nine years, the last committee meeting in connection with it being held on the 23d of April 1874, and the whole proceedings were finally brought to a close on the 8th of May 1874, when a supper took place in the Castle Campbell Hotel, a company of twenty gentlemen being present on the occasion.

The original committee had from time to time the following gentlemen added to its number :—Dr. John Strachan, Mr. James Christie, Mr. Symmers, Mr. Henry Cadogan, Mr. Charles Davies, Mr. T. S. Bradshaw, Mr. J. B. Henderson, all of whom seem to have taken a very active part, along with the original members of committee, in devising means to raise money for the extinction of the large debt entailed by the construction of the walk.

Some idea may be formed of the labour of Mr. Bradshaw in connection with it, when I state that no fewer than seventy-seven meetings were held from first to last, the minutes of some of which are of very great length ; and that, besides, a very extensive correspondence had been carried on between the committee and the several parties interested, the whole of which is engrossed in the minute-book.

The debt was wholly extinguished, and a small balance of £1, 5s. 9½d. left over, which was given to a few of the poor people of Dollar.

GRANT OF WATER TO DOLLAR.

When finished with this account of the making of this really most romantic walk to Castle Campbell, I think it would not be out of place here to refer to an undertaking that has been a great boon to Dollar, and *that* was the successful introduction of a bountiful supply of fine pure water from Dollar Glen, which must have proved an inestimable blessing to the village. The inhabitants of Dollar are under a deep debt of gratitude to the late Sir Andrew Orr for giving them a free grant in perpetuity of this abundant supply of fine water, and thus freeing them for ever from an expensive water-rate.

It used to be considered one of our great school-boy feats to go up Kemp's Score, and, in company with George Gibson (a son of the janitor's of the Academy), I accomplished it once, but was never tempted to try it again. My companion got fairly stuck for a time, and could neither get up nor down; and, considering all further efforts fruitless for that day, bawled up to me at the top, to go down and tell his folks to send up his supper, as it was evident to him he must remain there all night. However, by a last, almost despairing effort, he got over the difficulty, and reached the top in safety.

Our worthy minister, the late Dr. Andrew Mylne, had the misfortune to make a slip at the top of 'The Score,' and slid all the way down to the bottom on his back; and the wonder to every one was how he wasn't killed on the spot. As it was, he was very much hurt, and his nether garments were in a woful plight.

A young lady, also, from a neighbouring village, when visiting the Castle along with two gentlemen, had ventured down a little bit at the top of 'The Score,' and she, too, shared the same fate as the Doctor, and was so seriously hurt that she was confined to bed for a considerable time after it.

Whether Kemp's Score was a natural chasm, or one quarried out by the inhabitants of the Castle, I suppose no one can tell; but it must have been of great service to them when the Castle was besieged, as by it—if provided by wooden steps (as it would very likely be)—a supply of water could at all times be got, independently of their enemies.

I used often to imagine that part of the ground below the Castle garden had a hollow sort of sound, and that possibly some subterranean rooms might be in existence there; but no exploration of it was ever made, although I think it might yet be worth while doing so. Perhaps some antiquarian friend may persuade Mr. Orr to take the matter up.

Mr. and Mrs. John Taylor, and a large family, lived for a very long time in the Castle, in the two rooms at the foot of the stair, which must have been a very dismal abode to live in; but they were all very strong and healthy-looking notwithstanding, and seemed to get on quite comfortably in them. Looking at the whole place and its surroundings, it is really a mystery how some of the children didn't get themselves killed.

A family is at present living in the Castle, but the accommodation for them has been very much improved and enlarged since John Taylor's time. The danger, however, for children is as great as ever, and must keep the parents very anxious.

The Castle was thoroughly repaired in 1874-75, by the present proprietor, James Orr, Esq., and may now stand for very many centuries. Previous to this it was fast crumbling into decay, and in the course of another hundred years would probably have been a shapeless mass of ruins. The internal accommodation also, for the family who live in it, has been greatly enlarged and improved, and no more picturesque spot could be got anywhere for summer quarters.

PORTGOBER.

The hamlet of Pitgober, about a mile east from Dollar, and not far from the Vicar's Bridge, was called, it is said, Portgober in days of old, and an anchor, tradition says, was once discovered there, deeply imbedded in the soil. Whether this be a myth or not, there cannot be a doubt but that at one time (although at a considerably remote period) the whole valley of the Devon and the carse lands of Clackmannan and Stirlingshire were covered to a great depth by the waters of the ocean, and that most probably vessels would regularly trade to the inland seaport of Portgober. In that most interesting book, *Ossian on the Clyde*, the Rev. Hateley Waddell clearly proves that the whole valley of the Clyde was at one time an arm of the sea, and that where Govan and the lower parts of the city of Glasgow now stand, it was covered to a great depth with water; and that probably small boats and vessels of light draught could then sail from Ardrishaig to Crinan without the aid of a canal. If this, then, was the case on the west coast, it would, of course, be the same on the east, and the towns and villages of those days must have been at a very much higher level than at present.

That this was the case is established beyond the possibility of doubt, from the fact that the skeleton of a whale, sixty-four feet long, was discovered on Cornton Farm, near Bridge of Allan; and about seventy years ago one of seventy-two feet long was found in the ' Moss Park,' on Airthrey estate, not far from Logie Church, and this park has ever since been known by the name of the ' Whale Park.' This latter whale is only six feet shorter than the skeleton of the one in the Museum in Edinburgh, which is seventy-eight feet long, and which was caught, stranded on the beach near North Berwick, in the year 1826.

On the authority of those who live in the neighbourhood, there is said to be a very old rusted ring in the front of the 'Yellow Craig,' above Logie Church, to which, tradition says, vessels in those ancient times had been moored; but I have not seen it myself, although a guide in Blairlogie offered one day to take me to it, if I had had time, which unfortunately that day I had not. It is very doubtful, however, that it really was used for this purpose, as I am afraid iron could not last so long exposed to the action of the atmosphere. Sea shells, however, have been dug up on the top of the 'Yellow Craig,' which shows the sea to have been at one time there.

Two very worthy brothers, Mr. James and Mr. Adam Hutton, lived in Pitgober in my young days, and a great intimacy existed between them and my father's family. Mr. James worked a small farm, and many a happy night we spent in his house at the 'Harvest Home,' or 'Maiden,' as we used to call it. His son William served an apprenticeship in my father's shop, and afterwards commenced a wholesale business in Glasgow, in the prosecution of which he travelled through the greater part of England, and pushed very hard to establish a business for himself. He was cut off, however, when quite a young man. Mr. Adam Hutton was factor for some of the small proprietors around, and in this capacity acted for a great number of years for Dr. Paton of Lawhill and Middletown. Mr. Adam was a bachelor, and lived with his brother. Their house was the farthest west of the little village.

Another well-known inhabitant of Pitgober in those days was Mr. Charles Stewart (Charlie Stewart he used generally to be called), a very pushing small farmer.

Charles was 'excellent company,' and I have a very distinct recollection of a curlers' dinner in the Castle Campbell Hotel, at which he acted as one of the croupiers, and kept us all in good humour the whole evening.

COLLIERIES.

Extensive and valuable seams of coal underlie the whole of Dollar parish, and further east into that of Muckart, and forty to fifty years ago were extensively wrought. Dollar in those days had a considerable mining population, and Carbo, in the old town, was built specially for the colliers. It is as far back as I can recollect of the Fiddlefield coal-pit being wrought, which was the nearest pit to the village. Some of the seams of coal crop up to very near the surface, and, it was said, the folks used to hear the sound of the picks in below their houses when this pit was wrought. This I can readily believe, for in Tillicoultry Burn, adjoining Castle Mills, the coal actually comes up to the surface, and could be got in considerable quantity with very little trouble in digging.

The Middletown coal-pit was carried on very successfully for a great many years by Mr. Maxton, with Mr. Snowdowne as his manager, and the row of houses just under it was then built. The Apple-yard pit, too, near to Kellybank, was also carried on for a long number of years.

At the same time that Mr. Maxton had the Dollar coal, he was lessee of the Tillicoultry coal-pits (the Woodlands, etc.) as well; and when he left the district, Mr. Snowdowne became lessee, and continued so for a good many years. They are now in the hands of the Alloa Coal Company.

When the Devon Iron-Works were in operation (near to Sauchie Old Tower), the ironstone mines at Vicar's

Bridge were extensively wrought; but the long cartage between the two places must have been a serious item of expense, and have added greatly to the cost of the finished iron. The mineral water got in these mines was at one time quite celebrated throughout the kingdom for its healing properties, and sent to all parts of the country. This was discovered from one of the miners having got a severe flesh wound, which was quickly healed by working amongst the water. The entrance to these mines is now entirely closed up. Now that the railway has got within a few hundred yards of them, however, they may again probably be opened up.

A good story is told in connection with the Middletown coal-pit. A Mr. Lachlan M'Intosh (or 'old Lachie,' as he used to be called), an Excise officer in Dollar, got frequently and seriously 'on the spree,' and was a well-known character in the district. Well, in one of his drunken 'bouts' he had somehow wandered down the stair of this coal-pit, and, lying down on the stair, fell sound asleep. On some of the colliers coming up from their work, Lachie was discovered, and, a happy thought striking them, he was at once hoisted on one of their backs, and carried down into the workings. After sleeping off his carousal, he was horrified to find himself, on awaking, in some dreadful place of darkness, with lights flitting about in all directions, and was at once seized with the most dreadful forebodings. Coming forward at the moment, a black creature, with a light on its head, paused before him, and in stern language demanded, 'Who are you, sir?' when Lachie dolefully replied, 'I was a gauger in the last world, but I dinna ken what a'm gaun to be in this.' We can easily imagine what a relief it would be to him when he got back to *terra firma* again.

CHAPTER II.

WILSON FAMILY OF BANKHEAD, AND LETTERS FROM AMERICA
DURING THE AMERICAN WAR IN 1812 AND 1813.

IN the old churchyard of the county town of Clackmannan, a tombstone is to be seen not far from the
east end of the church, the inscription on which runs
as follows:—

1828.
Erected by SARAH WILSON
in memory of
Her dear departed friends,
SARAH MALLOCH, her Grandmother,
died 1st July 1791, aged 73 ;
ALEXANDER WILSON, her Grandfather,
died 18th April 1806, aged 72 ;
ANNIE, her Sister, died 20th Feby.
1814, aged 13 ;
HENRY, her Brother, died 9th Augt.
1828, aged 33 ;

Also the above
SARAH WILSON, died 24th Decr. 1861, aged 79.

'Come, here is mouldering dust;
behold and see
what you and I and all ere
long must be.'

This Alexander Wilson and Sarah Malloch are my
maternal great-grandfather and great·grandmother.

Standing at the Cross of Clackmannan, and looking up the only street of which the town consists, their house is the first one on the right-hand side, with an outside stone stair.

How many of a family they had I have not been able to learn; but they had one daughter, named Mary, who married a cousin of her own—Adam Wilson, who was laird of the farm of Bankhead, in Fossoway parish. They had a family of nine children—six sons and three daughters—their names and the years of their birth being as follows:—

William Wilson,	born in 1781.
Sarah Wilson,	,, 1782.
Robert Wilson,	,, 1786.
Mary Wilson (my mother),	,, 1788.
Adam Wilson,	,, 1790.
Alexander Wilson,	,, 1792.
Henry Wilson,	,, 1795.
Bruce Wilson,	,, 1798.
Annie Wilson,	,, 1800.

Uncle William, the eldest son, emigrated in 1801 to America, and established himself as a market gardener in the city of New York. He died about the year 1833, leaving a large family, none of whom, however, we have ever seen. His eldest son corresponded with my brother in Dollar, and thought at one time of coming over to see us, but never made it out. He died some years ago. We know nothing of his family, or of any of the other members of uncle's family. From three letters of uncle's that have just been put into my hands by my brother in Dollar (written in 1812 and 1813), I find he had been a most intelligent and really good man, and gifted, withal, with a poetical turn of mind of no mean order.

Two of these letters were written to his sister Sarah, and one to his young brother Henry, then only sixteen years of age, and are of general interest, from the fact that they were written during the American war with Britain, and show very clearly the great difficulty there was in carrying on any intercourse or correspondence between the two countries at that time. The following quotations will show this. In a letter to his sister, dated June 1813, he says : ' I am sorry that the war between this country and Britain should interrupt our correspondence, yet I expect to have frequent opportunities by the Cartel ships to write you ; and although such letters are all examined by the officers of the Government, and no doubt will be so long as the war continues, yet our correspondence being perfectly inoffensive is no detriment in the least to them. This, and another for Sandy, go by the Cartel ship *Robert Burns*, from New York to Liverpool. Mr. Gibb in Dunfermline will be able to inform you how to get your letters properly conveyed for the Cartel ships, which are the only chance now by which we can write.' Again, in another letter to his sister, dated December 24th, 1813, he says : ' Your kind letter of last July and the other two, sent by the return of the *Robert Burns*, I received all safe. May God grant that we may be equally prosperous with the present Cartel.'

And again in the same letter he says : ' I send one letter to Sandy along with this by the Cartel ship *Fair American*, bound to Liverpool, where she will be allowed to remain but a short time before her return to the United States. It is of no consequence to what port any of the Cartel ships come here ; their letters are very speedily forwarded to New York from any port in the Union. There was one, the *Minerva*, that arrived at

Boston not long ago from Leith. It would have been a fine opportunity for Sandy, and I wondered he did not write by her.'

Having been informed by his sister of the death of his mother at Bankhead, Fossoway, those two letters to her, from which I have quoted, are full of expressions of the most intense, glowing love to his dear departed mother, for whom he and all the family seemed to have entertained the deepest love and affection. In one of them he wishes a white marble tombstone to be erected to her memory, with the following inscription, the expense of which was to be entirely borne by himself :—

Sacred

to the memory of

M A R Y   W I L S O N,

wife of ADAM WILSON, of

Bankhead, of Tullybole,

who departed this life on the

27th day of June 1812, aged 52 years.

This stone is erected by her affectionate children, as a lasting testimony of that sincere regard which they bear for the memory of the best of mothers.

The last sad tribute they can here bestow for that maternal and affectionate regard invariably manifested by her unsullied bosom for the best interests of her darling offspring.

———

'Blessed are the dead who die in the Lord.'

The death of his mother, and a number of their neighbours, at Bankhead about the same time, suggested to him the following lines, which I here give as a specimen of his poetry :—

' But lately I roamed through yon bonnie green valley,
　The fields they were wet with the soft morning dew,
And the sweet native notes of the lark still ascended,
　Far on high rose her song as still upward she flew.

' My mind it was cheered by the sweet-smelling verdure
　　Of all that is fair in kind nature's display,
The full-blown flowers wide their glories expanded,
　　The rose and the lily bloomed fragrant and gay.

' Green were the boughs of the high towering forest,
　　Brave emblems of virtue they soared still on high,
Their sweet-smelling odours spread o'er the valley,
　　Their exalted perfume reached the far-distant sky.

' Though my feet wandered wide to yon far-distant nation,
　　My soul hovered still o'er the midst of the vale ;
Deep, deep in my bosom lay hid the sweet treasure,
　　Instilled from the fairest, the dearest of all.

' With fond exultation how joyful I tasted
　　Of these sweets,* though far wafted across the wide sea ;
But ah ! how short-lived are our best earthly treasures,
　　The *beauty* of Foss'way blooms no more for me !

' The greatest, the fairest of all the green forest—
　　How stately they flourished, how pleasant they shone !—
Are laid low in the dust, in silence they moulder ;
　　The *glory of Fossoway* is fallen, is gone.

' Where are her cedars that waved on the mountain ?
　　How does her forest look scanty and thin !
O chilly blast, had thou spared but the fairest,
　　The *bonnie white lily*, how glad had I been !

' Her old goodly timber that still stands unshaken,
　　Both cheerless and dreary alone now remain ;
O soft be the breeze that may ever pass o'er them ;
　　Pleasant and calm be their last setting sun.

' Ye dear tender shoots who are now thus exposed,
　　Unsheltered to feel the rough tempest's cold blast,
O how I would lock you to this warm bosom,
　　And hide thee in safety within this fond breast !

' Nor time nor great distance shall e'er dim those features,
　　Of love and affection my soul ever warms ;
It pores o'er the valley with filial raptures,
　　It lingers, it strays by the dearest of urns.'

---

* His mother's most affectionate letters.

In a footnote under this poetry he says: 'Two lines of the first verse allude to the early morning prayers of our worthy mother, and the two next verses to the happy situation of those who lived under the auspicious care of her, and the other worthy friends that are gone.'

That this poetical turn of mind was not confined to him alone of the family, may be gathered from the following quotation from the same letter, written immediately after the poetry:—

'In the above verses I have followed the same imagery as that in which my little brother Henry had been traversing. His verses I carefully copied from your letter, and, for a youth of sixteen, I think them well composed.'

From the whole letter to his brother Henry, he shows himself to have been a decided Christian, and the many excellent counsels contained in it, and the language in which they are expressed, would have done credit to any minister. Throughout all the three letters he shows the greatest interest in the temporal and eternal welfare of all his brothers and sisters, and in one of them refers to my father and mother (who were then only about a year married), as 'our brother Gibson and Mary.'

The many excellent advices given to his young brother in the letter to him are so suitable for young lads about to start on the business of life, that I think I cannot do better than give a few extracts from it, for the benefit of the rising generation of the present day. Although written seventy years ago (the letter being dated September 20th, 1812), they are as suitable now as they were then. In it he says:—

'You will scarcely remember the man that thus

addresses you; yet often, often do I think of the playful scenes you gratified me with in your youngest years. But now that you are grown up, considerations of far more importance will no doubt occupy your thoughts; and as all men continually stand in need of, and are greatly benefited by, serious and sound admonitions, I send you this letter with a sincere desire that it may prove a lasting blessing to you, and that you may not be without a memorandum of a brother who sincerely loves you.   Whatever your inclinations may be respecting the occupation you intend to follow, happiness is undoubtedly the grand object of all your wishes; yet perfect happiness cannot be obtained on this side the grave.   But there is an inexpressible happiness to be obtained which the "worldly-minded" knows not of, neither can the world give, or take it away.

'Let me advise you above all things to hold daily and frequent intercourse with your Creator, and endeavour as far as possible to regulate all your conduct according to the good laws of God, so plainly exhibited to you in your Bible.   Perhaps you have already gone, or may soon go, to some trade.   Then, in a special manner, ought you to be on your guard.   Above all things, in your dealings with mankind, observe these two, truth and honesty, by which you will command respect from all who know you; whereas falsehood and covetousness justly incur the contempt of everybody.   All kinds of swearing and obscene language sadly demean the man, deprave his every virtue, and sink him below the level of the very brute.   Beware, I beseech you, of the friendship of those who indulge in every kind of wickedness and obscenity.   You will always find in every place some whose minds naturally rise above the vile and ignominious.   Such minds will ever warm to those of similar affections, and the improving intercourse that ensues is truly pleasing and useful.

'The man who spends his life without the society of a virtuous friend can scarcely know what it is to live. Such an one I hope you will always be able to enjoy, and may God ever preserve you from the paths of vice. . . .

'I send this letter, and one to Robert, with a Mr. Murphy, whose family lives in Paisley. He has been here a few months only, and returns in a Cartel ship to Liverpool. . . . He is much pleased with my situation.'

I find the postage of those letters was 2s. 6d., this sum being marked on the back of one of them. (There were no envelopes in those days, nor for many a day after—the letters being written on three sides of a big square sheet of paper, and addressed on the fourth.) It is also written on each of them when they were received, and in every case I find it took about two months for the packet to cross the Atlantic.

What a contrast to all this exists at the present day, and how would my worthy uncle be astonished could he revisit this earthly scene again! Instead of two months, his letters would now reach their destination in some seven or eight days, with unfailing regularity, driven along against wind and tide and the ocean currents of the Atlantic by that wonderful agent steam, the irresistible force of which was first discovered by James Watt, when he tied down the lid of the kettle, stopped up the spout, and blew away at the fire with the bellows, to see what effect it would have, when he escaped death as if by a miracle, the kettle being shivered to atoms.

And then, instead of looking out for friends by whom to send his letters, and when none could be got, sending them through the post office at a charge of 2s. 6d., we get them despatched daily now for the small sum of 2½d. only, by the magnificent fleet of gigantic steamers that now cross the Atlantic.

But how would uncle stare in utter amazement, when told that he could flash a message with lightning speed across the Atlantic to his sister in a few minutes, by a mysterious wire at the bottom of the ocean! Yet those are amongst the great advantages we now enjoy, as compared with his day, and for all of which, and for many other great discoveries since his time, we ought to be truly thankful.

He was the author of a very excellent book on gardening, published by Anderson, Davis, & Co., Chatham Square, New York, in 1828. It is entitled, '*Economy of the Kitchen-Garden, the Orchard, and the Vinery, with Plain Practical Directions for their Management.* By William Wilson, nurseryman.' It is a book of two hundred and six pages, and contains a very full treatise of the subject, and must have been invaluable in those early days of the settlement of the country. He had got the copyright of his book secured; and the fact that it was so is made known in the first page,—a short extract from which I here give as follows :—

'*Southern District of New York, S.S.*

'BE IT REMEMBERED, that on the sixteenth day of October, in the fifty-second year of the Independence of the United States of America, William Wilson, of the said district, hath deposited in this office the title of a book, the right whereof he claims as author and proprietor, in the words following, to wit :—

[Here follows the title, as given above.]

In conformity to the Act of the Congress of the United

States, entitled " An Act for the Encouragement of Learning, by securing the Copies of Maps, Charts, and Books to the Authors and Proprietors of such Copies, during the times therein mentioned. . . . And extending the Benefits thereof to the Arts of Designing, Engraving, and Etching Historical and other Prints."

'FREDERICK J. BETTS,
' *Clerk of the Southern District of New York.*'

It may not be uninteresting to give a copy of the index to the book, as showing what products were principally reared at that time in America. It is as follows :—

VEGETABLES.

Asparagus, bean, beet, broccoli, cabbage, cauliflower, celery, carrot, cucumber, corn salad, cress, endive, egg plant, garlick, horse bean, horseradish, Indian corn, kail, lettuce, leek, melon, New Zealand spinnage, nasturtium, onion, okra, parsnip, parsley, pea, pepper, pumpkin, potato, radish, spinage, squash, sorrel, salsify, shallot, turnip, tomato.

POT AND SWEET HERBS.

Caraway, coriander, sweet basil, summer savory, sage, thyme.

MEDICINAL HERBS.

Balm, calomile, comfrey, catmint, elecampane, horehound, hyssop, mint, rue, tansey, wormwood.

FRUIT.

Apple, pear, peach, plum, cherry, apricot, nectarine, quince, gooseberry, currant, raspberry, strawberry, grape vine.

Of the vine, he says the following sorts have been found to succeed tolerably well in America :—

Millen Burgundy, Golden Chasselas, White Chasselas, White Sweet Water, White Muscadine, Morillon Blanc, Black Hamburgh, Tokay, Blue Cartiga, Muscat Violet, Messlier, Austrian Muscadell.

From the introduction to his book I learn that, from a diary he kept regularly for a period of nine years of the results of all his various gardening operations, and from the experience gathered for twenty-seven years of what best suited the soil and climate in the neighbour-hood of New York, he had gathered the materials for another and more important work, which was imme-diately to follow his first one, the title of which was to be ' *The New York Horticulturist,*' and in which he says would be found ' a distinct arrangement of all the views of importance which I have formed and entertain respecting the practical execution of all the various operations necessary to be performed in the more refined departments of landscape gardening, the pleasure or flower garden, the hothouse, greenhouse, and forcing-frames. But as these subjects are not necessarily much connected with the kitchen garden, it has been thought better to commence with the manage-ment of it by itself, the more especially as it is presumed the far greater part of the purchasers will prefer to have it so. The management of fruit trees and grape vines being so nearly allied to that of the kitchen garden, they will be freely treated upon in the present work, as soon as we get our kitchen garden well cropped.'

Of this second work we have, unfortunately, no copy (so far as I know). The copy of the one from which I have been quoting was made a present of to my father by the author, and is inscribed on the first page, in his own handwriting, as follows :—

Presented to
WILLIAM GIBSON,
by his Brother,
THE AUTHOR.
New York, October 2, 1828.

It is now in the possession of one of my sisters.

As a contrast to those 'floating islands' that now leave Glasgow almost daily to cross the Atlantic, it may not be uninteresting here to refer to the *Comet*, the first steamer that was started on the Clyde, which was built in 1811, by J. Wood, for Henry Bell. It was only forty-two feet long, eleven feet broad, and five and a half feet deep.

This leviathan steamer was advertised to sail, in a newspaper dated 5th August 1812 ; and referring as it does to those early days of steam navigation, I here give a copy of it in full :—

'STEAM PASSAGE BOAT THE *Comet*, BETWEEN GLASGOW
AND HELENSBURGH, FOR PASSENGERS ONLY.

'The subscriber having at much expense fitted up a handsome vessel to ply upon the Clyde between Glasgow and Greenock, to sail by the power of wind, air, and steam, he intends that the vessel shall leave the Broomielaw on Tuesdays, Thursdays, and Saturdays about mid-day, or at such hour thereafter as may answer from the state of the tide ; and to leave Greenock on Mondays, Wednesdays, and Fridays in the morning to suit the tide. The elegance, comfort, safety, and speed of this vessel require only to be proved to meet the approbation of the public ; and the proprietor is determined to do everything in his power to merit public encouragement. The terms are for the present fixed at 4s. for the best cabin, and 3s. for the second; but beyond these rates nothing is to be allowed to servants or any other persons employed about the vessel. The subscriber continues his establishment at Helensburgh Baths the same as for ten years past, and a vessel will be in readiness to convey passengers in the *Comet* from Greenock to Helensburgh. Passengers by the *Comet* will receive information of the hours of sailing by applying at Mr. Houstan's office, Broomielaw, or Mr. Thomas Blackney, East Quay Head, Greenock.

'HENRY BELL.'

Aunt Sarah and Uncle Henry lived in their grandfather's house in Clackmannan, and carried on the little shop in connection with it. Uncle died at the early age of thirty-three, but aunt lived to the long age of seventy-nine.

Uncle Robert, who was a builder, established himself in Paisley, and his sons John, William, and Robert used frequently to visit us in Dollar. They have now emigrated to America.

Uncle Adam (who never was married) lived for long in Dollar, but latterly in Paisley, and died there.

Uncle Alexander emigrated to America, and we never heard where he settled, or what became of him.

Uncle Bruce was drowned in the Caldron Linn. No one saw him fall in; but a stepping-stone that used to be at the top of the upper fall, and by which people got across the Devon, was amissing, and this led to the supposition that he might have fallen in. This, alas! turned out to be too true; for, after a week's searching, his body was got in the lower pool.

W.Beck & son, Edin[r]

CALDRON LINN.

Aunt Annie died in my father's house, at the early age of thirteen. She was a good little girl, and told the friends around her deathbed that if she died on a Sabbath, to be sure she was in heaven. And on a Sabbath, sure enough, she did die.

THE OLD HOME IN DOLLAR.

I come now to the one of the family around whom the greatest interest centres — my dear and loving mother, Mary, who was married to my father on the 26th of April 1811, being then twenty-three years of age, my father being a year younger.

I was told by a Mrs. M'Ilwraith, who lived in Tillicoultry, and who died only a few months ago, aged ninety-five, that she knew my father and mother very well before they were married, and that it was at a marriage in Dollar they first saw each other. Be this as it may, my father was fortunate in getting one of the best of women for his partner in life, and who afterwards proved a most devoted and excellent mother to his large family; and whose memory will, till the day of my death, be deeply enshrined in my inmost heart.

They had twelve of a family, four sons and eight daughters, five of whom (two sons and three daughters) died in infancy. The names of the survivors were as follows—six of whom are still living :—

Jane (Jeanie), first Mrs. Peter Dalgleish, Stirling.

James, married Elizabeth, youngest daughter of Mr. William Archibald, Craigfoot, Tillicoultry.

Mary-Ann (Mrs. Archibald, Devonvale, Tillicoultry, and Cluny Bank, Forres).

William, married Jessie Christie, eldest daughter of Mr. James Prentice, Stirling.

Janet (Mrs. Kirk, Park House, Dollar).

Sarah.

Amelia (Emily) (Mrs. M'Leish, Free Church Manse, Methven).

In my father's house we were most thoroughly drilled in the use of the Scriptures and the Shorter Catechism, having to repeat (question about) the one half of the latter every Sabbath night, my father asking all the questions without a book. This thorough knowledge of the Catechism was at that time, I believe, very general, and was considered essential to salvation ; and in almost every household it was looked upon as of equal authority with the Bible. That it should have been so, is, I think, very much to be regretted, as some important things were left out of it that should have been in, and some were given a prominence to that had better have been out.

I trust this old ' Standard ' will—like the New Testament—soon be revised, and those glorious truths made known in it (*which are not at present*), that Christ tasted death for *every man* (Heb. ii. 9) ; and that God will have *all men* to be saved, and to come unto the knowledge of the truth (1 Tim. ii. 4). I would like, also, to see added to the already beautiful answer to the fourth question of, ' What is God,' those three precious words, ' *God is love* ' (1 John iv. 8). When referring to this fourth question of the Catechism, I think it would not be out of place here to give a short extract from a very beautiful address I saw lately, on the love of God, and the great mistake many people made regarding it. ' The great source of the mental anguish of thousands is caused by thinking that *they* must make God love them *by being good*. Now God loves us, *not* because *we are good*, but because He is *our Father*. The cross of Christ does not

make God love us; it is the outcome and measure of
His love to us. He loves *all* His children—the clumsiest,
the dullest, the ugliest, and the *worst*. His love lies at
the back of everything, and we must get upon that as
the solid foundation of our religious life, not growing up
into that, but growing up out of it.' No poor sin-
burdened soul, mourning over the wickedness and depravity of his or her sinful heart, need ever despair
when they see the love of their heavenly Father to them,
as manifested in the beautiful parable of the Prodigal
Son (Luke xv. 11). 'When he was yet *a great way off,*'
the father did not wait till he came to him, but ran and
met him, fell on his neck, kissed, and embraced his son;
showing clearly that God is at all times more willing to
receive us, than we are to go to Him.

When referring to this parable, an interesting story I
read a few years ago in one of the children's magazines,
has been brought to mind, and it may not be out of
place to introduce it here. A gentleman's son had lived
a very reckless, sinful life; and, after sinking lower and
lower in depravity, he was at last forced to join himself to other two or three kindred spirits, and perform
through the streets as a coloured minstrel. Stopping in
front of a shop door one day, the merchant (a godly
man) offered a shilling to this son if he would read aloud
to them all a portion of Scripture which he would point
out to him. The offer being gladly accepted, the Bible
was opened, and Luke xv. 11 having been pointed out
to him, he commenced at once to his task. He had not
proceeded far, when one of his companions ejaculated,
'*That's thee, Jim,*' and frequently, as he continued, repeated the exclamation; till at last the poor fellow fairly
broke down, and, like the son of whom he had been
reading, he resolved there and then that 'he would arise

and go to his father,' and confess all his past wickedness, and ask his forgiveness. He did so, and was welcomed back to his friends, and this good merchant's shilling proved the means, in God's hand, of this young prodigal's conversion.

There is no unwillingness on God's part that we should be saved, and we will have ourselves to blame if we are not so. He has provided an all-sufficient Saviour for us, if we will only accept of Him. He says : ' As I live, saith the Lord God, I have no pleasure in the death of the wicked ; but that the wicked turn from His way and live : turn ye, turn ye from your evil way, for *why* will ye die ? ' (Ezek. xxxiii. 11). And then we have what I look upon as the most precious verse in the whole Bible, John iii. 16, ' For God so loved *the world* that He gave His only-begotten Son, that *whosoever* believeth in Him should not perish, but have everlasting life.' What a precious word that ' *Whosoever* ' is—the poor broken-hearted penitent, the self-righteous Pharisee, the openly wicked and profane, all are here invited to come, and accept of this all-sufficient Saviour ; but we *must come,* and each for himself or herself, personally, accept of Him, for Jesus says in another place of those who reject Him, ' Ye will not come to me that ye might have life ' (John v. 40). How precious is this invitation : ' Come unto me, all ye that labour and are heavy laden, and I will give you rest. Take my yoke upon you, and learn of me ; for I am meek and lowly in heart: and ye shall find rest unto your souls. For my yoke is easy, and my burden is light ' (Matt. xi. 28, 29, 30). And again : ' Behold, I stand at the door, and knock : if *any man* hear my voice, and open the door, I will come in to him, and will sup with him, and he with me ' (Rev. iii. 20).

Let none, then, be afraid of being *shut out* from the atonement of Jesus, when they read those precious verses.

In personal appearance my father was about the average height (5 ft. 8 or 9 in.), with a full round face; and, for a long time before he died, had got very grey and bald. He was a kind and affectionate parent, and at the same time very strict in maintaining proper discipline in his household.

He always enjoyed a good story, and had a perfect fund of anecdotes himself, few of which, however, I am sorry to say, I can remember. He used to tell a very good one of a Mr. James Stewart, a gentleman boarder of the Rev. Mr. Brown's of Glendevon. Mr. Stewart, as Scotch folks would say, 'had a want,' but at the same time a degree of cleverness about him which at. times was very amusing. The Rev. George Graham of Fossoway used to preach occasionally for Mr. Brown, and was in the habit of teasing Mr. Stewart very much, which sadly annoyed him, and he resolved, quietly, that some day he would have his revenge. Well, one Sabbath day, when Mr. Graham was preaching for Mr. Brown, a favourable opportunity occurred. In finishing his sermon he shut the Bible, and said, 'I add no more;' when up started Mr. Stewart in front of the pulpit, and (having an impediment in his speech) bawled out, as loud as he could, in the hearing of the whole congregation, 'A—a—a—gude reason whey, Geordie lad, ye've nae mair te add.' We can easily conceive what 'a chuckle' would run through the congregation, and that Mr. Graham would not, after this, be in the best possible mood for finishing the rest of the service.

Many other amusing stories are told of Mr. Stewart by others, and, while referring to him, I may here give one or two I got from the Rev. John M'Leish, who knew him well. The Rev. John Clark of Blackford—like Mr. Graham—frequently preached for Mr. Brown, and he also, it seems, had taken a pleasure in teasing Mr. Stewart, and Jamie (as he used to be called) made up his mind that he would some day ' be upsides with him.' Mr. Stewart had made himself very useful in Glendevon Church, and regularly performed all the duties of the church-officer, ringing the bell, and taking the Bible up into the pulpit, etc. ; so that it was unnecessary to employ a paid official for these duties. Well, on one occasion, when Mr. Clark was going to officiate, Mr. Stewart got the sermon from him to put into the Bible, that he knew was going to be *read* to the folks that day (reading sermons in those days was not so common as it is now, and was looked upon with great disfavour by the people ; it being no uncommon occurrence, when a sermon was read, to see some one rise and go out), and away he marched up to the pulpit with the Bible ; and, in order to let the congregation see what they might expect, he opened the Bible, and held it up, first to the one gallery, and then to the other, showing off the minister's manuscript, accompanying it, no doubt, with some knowing ' winks ' and grimaces ; and while this performance was going on, Mr. Clark—rather sooner than was expected—walked into the church, and ' took in ' the whole situation at a glance ; when down went the Bible with a thump on the pulpit, and Jamie made ' clean heels ' down the pulpit stair, and out of the church, to the great amusement of the whole congregation, and the no little discomfiture of poor Mr. Clark.

It was a habit with Mr. Clark, when preaching, to lift the Bible from the pulpit, and lay it down, first on the one side, and then on the other, which was rather peculiar, and very noticeable. Well, at dinner that day (there being a goodly company present), Mr. Clark thought he would be revenged on Mr. Stewart for the insult he had offered him in the church, and was very severe with his satire upon the poor old man; when, without saying a single word, Mr. Stewart rose from the table, got hold of a big Bible, and, placing it down before him, commenced to turn it over from one side to the other, which fairly 'set the table in a roar,' and completely turned the laugh against his assailant.

When Mr. Stewart was from home he invariably put a half-crown in the plate on Sabbath days; but when at Blackford on one occasion he departed from his usual practice, and put in only a threepenny-bit—Mr. Clark having offended him in some way before going to church. When the collection was about to be counted (Mr. Stewart being present), Mr. Clark turned over the contents of the plate from side to side in search of the usual half-crown; and finding—to his great astonishment —only a threepenny-bit instead, he could not conceal his disappointment, and, turning to Mr. Stewart, said, 'What do you think the folks will be crying after you through the streets, but "Threepenny Jamie, Threepenny Jamie"?' when Mr. Stewart very coolly and amusingly replied, 'Will they, though? and what do you think they will cry after you, but "Paper Jock, Paper Jock";' which fairly convulsed the members of session with laughter, and scored another complete triumph for Mr. Stewart. I should think that Mr. Clark would, after this, be glad to let poor Jamie alone.

I will now give just one other anecdote about him, although many others could be told. When at Blackford on one sacramental occasion, Mr. Clark—being rather scarce of elders that day—asked Mr. Stewart if he would stand at the plate at the church door, to which he at once agreed. As usual on these occasions, services were being conducted at a tent in the churchyard, and, the day being fine, the great bulk of the people preferred going to the tent, instead of into the church. The result of this was, that while the plate for the tent congregation was well filled, Jamie's was almost empty; so, watching a favourable opportunity,—when the elder at the tent plate was temporarily absent,—he slipped quietly over to it, carried and emptied it into the church-door plate, and then replaced the empty plate in its old position. We can easily fancy the consternation of the elder when he returned and found his plate empty; and his first thought would, I daresay, be to cry for the police, had there been any such officials in that part of the world. However, after a little calm reflection, he would not, I daresay, be at a great loss to suspect who had been the rogue, when he remembered that Mr. Stewart was there that day.

I recollect Mr. Stewart's appearance very well. He was a man well up in years, and, being slightly paralyzed on one side, had a limp in walking, and stooped considerably to that side.

[George Brown (a son of the Rev. Mr. Brown's with whom Mr. Stewart boarded) was one of my most intimate school companions.]

Photography not having been discovered in my father's day, the only likeness we have of him was taken, in pencil, by one of the candidates for the drawing-master's situation in Dollar Academy, when Mr. Brown was appointed. My father being one of the trustees of the Institution, this candidate wished to show him what he could do; and hence this portrait. I am very sorry we have no likeness whatever of my mother; but, had I been an artist, I think I could take her portrait yet, her features are so indelibly impressed on my memory, although very young when she died. It was on the 29th of August 1828 that this sad event took place, which brought a dark cloud over us all, and brought their married life to a termination after the short sojourn together of only seventeen years.

Although so young when this sad event happened, I have—as already stated—a distinct recollection of her sweet and loving face, and only those who have experienced, like myself, what it is to lose a loving partner in life, can have any idea of the irreparable loss my father sustained in the death of his young wife (she was only forty), and what a loss it must have been to her young family.

This great blow (the greatest, I think, that can befall us poor mortals here below) would weigh on my father's spirits till the day of his death; for however full your house may be, your companion is gone, and nothing on earth can make up for the loss. He nevertheless bore up wonderfully under it, and apparently was always cheerful when in the presence of any one, and enjoyed a quiet meeting of friends very much. But 'the heart knoweth its own bitterness;' and (speaking from. my own experience) solitude is found at times to be a great relief, where the pent-up fountain of our grief can flow out freely, unrestrained by the presence of any one. In the words of another, 'Hearts constitute homes, and the loss of a beloved wife is the communion of home ended, and the husband left to a solitude that no tears can relieve, no entreaties reverse.' Seven of a family (one more than in my own case) were left with him to mourn over the loss of his partner in life.

Our heavenly Father has wise ends in view in those great trials He sends upon us, and though we cannot see through them now, we shall be able to comprehend them in eternity, and to then realize that 'all things work together for good to those who love the Lord.' Those great bereavements are—amongst other things—sent to try our faith, and I think I cannot do better than here introduce one of Spurgeon's beautiful *Morning by Morning Readings* (a precious book), bearing on this subject. It is on October 7, from Num. xi. 11 : 'Wherefore hast Thou afflicted Thy servant?' 'Our heavenly Father sends us frequent troubles to try our faith. If our faith be worth anything, it will stand the test. Gilt is afraid of fire, but gold is not ; the paste gem dreads to be touched by the diamond, but the true jewel fears no test. It is a poor faith which can only trust God when friends are true, the body full of health, and the business profitable ; but that is true faith which holds by the Lord's faithfulness when friends are gone, when the body is sick, when spirits are depressed, and the light of our Father's countenance is hidden. A faith which can say, in the direst trouble, "Though He slay me, yet will I trust in Him," is heaven-born faith. The Lord afflicts His servants to glorify Himself, for He is greatly glorified in the graces of His people, which are His own handiwork. When "tribulation worketh patience ; and patience, experience ; and experience, hope," the Lord is honoured by these growing virtues. We should never know the music of the harp if the strings were left untouched ; nor enjoy the juice of the grape if it were not trodden in the wine-press ; nor discover the sweet perfume of the cinnamon if it were not pressed and beaten ; nor feel the warmth of fire if the coals were not utterly consumed. The wisdom and

power of the great Workman are discovered by the
trials through which His vessels of mercy are permitted
to pass. Present afflictions tend also to heighten future
joy. There must be shades in the picture to bring out
the beauty of the lights. Could we be so supremely
blessed in heaven, if we had not known the curse of sin
and the sorrow of earth? Will not peace be sweeter
after conflict, and rest more welcome after toil? Will
not the recollection of past sufferings enhance the bliss
of the glorified? There are many other comfortable
answers to the question with which we opened our
brief meditation; let us muse upon it all day long.'

REFORM BILL OF 1832.

Although my father took no active public part in
politics, he was thoroughly Liberal in his views, and
when the great Reform Bill passed in 1832, was
amongst those who rejoiced that this first grand step
in the political regeneration of this country was taken.
Although very young at the time, I remember well the
great rejoicings that took place throughout the length
and breadth of the land. There was a great procession
at Dollar, with some seven or eight bands of music, and
we marched round by Rack-Mill, Dollarbeg, and Blairingone, and home by Vicar's Bridge. A public dance
also took place on the Brewer's Knowe.

In case some of my young readers may not know
what the Reform Bill was, I may here state that prior
to 1832 Scotland had no real representation whatever.
The *county* qualification of Scotland was limited to a
peculiar description of property, and was above a
hundred times higher than the corresponding qualifica-

tion in England,—the smallest English county containing as many voters as all the counties of Scotland put together. The condition of the *burghs* was different from, but not better than, that of the counties. The appointment of members of Parliament in burghs lay with the Town Councils, which were self-elected, and, as a rule, not well qualified for such an important responsibility,—the result being that the representation of the Scottish people in their own House was a mockery and a sham. By the Reform Act of 1832, the *county* qualifications were an occupancy franchise of £50, and an ownership one of £10 ; while in *burghs* the qualification was £10 for the proprietors and tenants. These qualifications continued until 1867, since which date every householder in burghs has a vote ; and in counties the ownership qualification has been £5, and that of occupants £14. There can be little doubt, however, that before the present Parliament is dissolved the present household qualification of burghs will have been extended to counties. The country is now in earnest that this change should take place, and no Parliament can long dare to withhold it.

The Reform Bill of 1832 was the first ' knock on the head ' our Tory legislators got, and put an end, to a great extent, to the ' class ' legislation which had been carried on for so long a period.

The first great contest in the united counties of Clackmannan and Kinross, to represent them in Parliament, after the passing of the Reform Bill, was between the late W. P. Adam's father, Admiral Adam (Liberal), and the present Lord Balfour of Burleigh's father, Mr. Bruce of Kennet (Tory), and resulted in a great victory for the Admiral, who was carried shoulder-high through Dollar.

CHAPTER III.

CAPTAIN JOHN M'NAB AND HIS SPLENDID BEQUEST
TO DOLLAR.

IN the year 1799 a message came one day to Mr.
M'Arbrea, the parish teacher of Dollar, that a gentleman
wished to see him in the village inn at Gateside; and
on repairing thither he found an entire stranger awaiting
him, who did not introduce himself, but who, in the
course of a long conversation, asked all the information
about Dollar that a parish teacher was so well qualified
to give; and, after getting this, bade Mr. M'Arbrea good-
bye, leaving him still in ignorance as to who his
interrogator was. He gave him to understand, however,
that the object of his inquiries was, that some one was
going to benefit the parish in an educational point of
view; and the inhabitants of Dollar are certainly very
much indebted to the shrewd old schoolmaster for
representing matters in such a light, that what this
stranger contemplated would be a very great boon and
blessing to Dollar, and would be highly prized by the
parishioners. This visit would no doubt give rise to a
good deal of talk in Dollar at the time, and great
curiosity would be excited as to who this inquisitive
gentleman was; but it was fully two years before the
mystery was cleared up, and after the visit had been
almost entirely forgotten. The first light that was
thrown on the incident was the intimation that came to

Dollar in 1802, that a Captain John M'Nab had died in London, leaving a large sum of money for ' a charity or school for the poor of the parish,' and it was to be under the management of the parish minister and kirk-session. This gentleman, then, had no doubt been Mr. M'Arbrea's mysterious visitor, and it became a settled point in Dollar, about which there need not be the slightest doubt.

As is well known, this Mr. John M'Nab, whose noble gift has so entirely changed the quiet little country village into the important place of learning it now is, was a native of Dollar parish, having been born at Wellhall, and was baptized in the Parish Church of Dollar on the 14th of May 1732—one hundred and fifty years ago. He left Dollar, when a young lad, for a seafaring life, and was so poor he had to borrow the three-halfpence necessary to take him across the Queen's Ferry, when on his way to Leith. From this time till he appeared again in Dollar in 1799 (which must have been some fifty years at least), he was entirely lost sight of, and would be—but by a very few—entirely forgotten. Having been successful in amassing a large fortune, and remembering, no doubt, the disadvantages under which he had himself laboured when a poor boy in Dollar, he had bethought himself of doing something for his native village ; and hence his splendid bequest.

The Rev. John Watson appears to have treated the people of Dollar very cavalierly ; for although the Rev. Noah Hill's letter to him, intimating Mr. M'Nab's bequest, was dated the 18th of January 1802, he appears not to have brought it before his session till the 2nd of March 1803, on which date it is taken notice of for the first time in the session records, and the will and Rev. Noah Hill's letter recorded.

On the 17th March 1803 a session meeting was held. Present with the Moderator, the Rev. John Watson, Messrs. James Gibson, James Christie, John Jack, Andrew Paton, and Robert Smith, elders.

On account of the doubtful wording of Mr. M'Nab's will, this meeting decided to take opinion of counsel regarding it, and the following letter was agreed to be sent to James Ferrier, W.S., Edinburgh, Commissioner to the Duke of Argyle :—

'DOLLAR, 17th March 1803.

' SIR,—*Inter alia*, the members of the kirk-session, on account of the doubtful wording of the will, wish to know whether they could advance the money requisite for managing the matter in the first instance out of the poor funds belonging to the parish, or if it is to be at their own risk, as none of them can afford it ; and, besides, it is no benefit to themselves, being a public and parochial concern ; or would you take the risk upon yourself, on being handsomely rewarded on obtaining a decision corroborating the will ? Your opinion as to either of these is expected by, sir, etc.,

' JOHN M'ARBREA.'

From this time till 1807 there appears to have been no session meetings held in connection with it, and both the heritors and inhabitants of Dollar were kept in entire ignorance of what Mr. Watson was doing in regard to the matter. Mr. M'Nab's executors having meanwhile raised a Chancery suit (the will being disputed by his cousin), the Court of Chancery ordered the kirk-session to exhibit a scheme of the mode in which they meant to dispose of the legacy. Mr. Watson, in compliance with this order, prepared one for erecting

a large hospital or poor-house, and did so apparently
without consulting his session, knowing that Mr.
M'Arbrea, the session-clerk, and, indeed, all the inhabitants of the parish, and heritors, were quite opposed to
this, and in favour of an educational seminary. (The
Chancery suit terminated in favour of Dollar.) As
soon as it got to be known that Mr. Watson had presented this scheme, a meeting of the heritors took place
on the 27th of January 1808, and also one of the inhabitants of the parish on the same day, with the view
of opposing it. Through the kindness of Mr. Haig of
Dollarfield, I am enabled to give a copy of the minutes
of both of those meetings, and the names of those who
attended them, which are as follow :—

'Minute of a meeting of the heritors of the parish of
Dollar, called to consider a plan which the minister of
the parish is stated to have presented, with the concurrence of the elders, to the Court of Chancery, for
erecting an hospital for poor children with Captain
M'Nab's legacy—held at Dollar the 27th day of January
1808.
'*Present*—Craufurd Tait, Esq. of Harviestoun, for himself, and Colonel Campbell, of Dollarbeg; John Duncanson, of Sheardale; William Fult, of Mains of Dollar;
William Haig, of Dollarfield; Robert Marshall, of Mains
of Dollar; Robert Pitcairn, in Dollar; John M'Cathie,
in Dollar; Thomas Lamb, of Mains of Dollar; James
Fergus, of Mains of Dollar; Walter Moir, for John Moir,
of Hillfoot.—Mr. Tait appointed *Preses*; Mr. Moir appointed *Clerk.*
'The meeting having very fully considered the subject,
are unanimously of opinion that the erection of an
hospital for poor children in the parish would be a great
misfortune, would discourage industry, and would tend
to bring into the parish a number of poor people; and
they resolve to oppose the erection of an hospital by

every means in their power, and, if necessary, to appear in the Court of Chancery and state the misfortunes which they consider it will bring upon the parish. Mr. Tait, Mr. Moir, and Mr. Haig stated to the meeting that when they heard that the minister and elders had made an application to the Court of Chancery for the establishment of an hospital or poor-house, they had retained counsel, and employed a solicitor to oppose the plan of the minister and elders. All the heritors and proprietors present approved of this, and authorized their names to be used in opposing the erection of an hospital or poor-house. They further resolved, and they individually obliged themselves, not to feu, or let, or in any way to give possession of any part of their grounds to the minister and elders for the erection of an hospital or poor-house, or an establishment of any kind with Mr. M'Nab's legacy, except a free school, which they think would promote the industry and prosperity of the parish.'

'Minutes of a meeting of the inhabitants of Dollar, called to consider a plan which the minister of the parish is stated to have presented, with the concurrence of the elders, to the Court of Chancery, for erecting an hospital for poor children with Captain M'Nab's legacy—held at Dollar the 27th day of January 1808.

'*Present* — William Donaldson, quarrier in Dollar; William Fyfe, coalmaster in Dollar; Alexander Hamilton, baker in Dollar; Andrew Sharp, smith in Dollar; William Gibson, flesher in Dollar; Francis Sharp, flesher in Dollar; Alexander Paterson, farmer in Dollarbeg; James Millar, mason in Dollar; John Maitland, Excise officer in Dollar; Robert Malcolm, mason in Dollar; Robert Leslie, carrier in Dollar; James Scott, overseer at Mains of Dollar.

'The minutes of the heritors of this day regarding the application of Captain M'Nab's legacy having been read to the meeting, and the persons present having both now and formerly considered the subject with all the attention in their power, they are unanimously of opinion that the erection of a free school, at which the different useful branches of education would be taught, would be the greatest blessing that could be conferred on the parish. As to the establishment of an hospital for poor children, they are of opinion that it would be an improper mode of applying Captain M'Nab's legacy, —first, because the number of children that could be admitted into such an hospital would be so small that it would not be of extensive benefit to the inhabitants of the parish.

'Secondly, because they consider that the greatest comfort which parents can receive is the company and conversation of their children in their own families; and they would be obliged to remove this comfort before their children could get the benefit of being educated in the hospital. Besides, they consider it their duty as parents to watch over the health and morals of their children, and they think that these will be as well attended to under their own eyes, as when they are trusted to a hired housekeeper, or hired servants in an hospital.

'Thirdly, from their early prejudices and education, they have been accustomed to consider it as their pride to be able to feed and clothe their children without the assistance of charity; and the consequence of the erection of an hospital would be either that they, the present inhabitants, would feel themselves degraded if they suffered their children to go into the hospital, and the minister and elders would be obliged to invite families from neighbouring parishes, with different feelings, to furnish children for filling the hospital.

'*Signed*—
William Donaldson.
James Millar.
William Fyfe.
William Gibson.
James Scott.
David Smitton.
Peter M'Nicol.
Andrew Robertson.

'*Signed*—
David Drysdale.
Francis Sharp.
Robert Younger.
John Carmichael.
Andrew Sharp.
James Lawson.
John Chalmers.
William Lyon.

'Signed—

John Brown.
James Donovan.
Daniel M'Gregor.
John Blackwood.
Alexander Patterson.
Alexander Hamilton.
Robert Leslie.
John Maitland.
Robert Malcolm.
Thomas Campbell.
Andrew Henderson.
Donald M'Laren.
Joseph Marshall.
Andrew Wilkie.
William Wilson.
James Blackwood.
William Blackwood.
John Blackwood.
George Thompson.
Duncan Cameron.
John Oliphant.
Hugh Munro.
William Monteath.
John Cameron.
John Taylor.
John Strang.
John Hynd.
William Duncan.
William Anderson.
Peter Campbell.
James Smith.
John Kirk.
John Drysdale.
Henry Wardlaw.
John Bateson.
John Burns.
John M'Lean.
John M'Leish.
Andrew Mallach.
David Wilson.
John Bowie.
John Ross.
William Reid.

'Signed—

Robert Wright.
William Carmichael.
John Drysdale.
William Halley.
Henry Murray.
John Younger.
Robert Jack.
Thomas Younger.
Peter Lawson.
Andrew Gray.
John Hall.
Joseph Sharp.
James Johnston.
Robert Lambert.
John M'Intosh.
Peter M'Leish.
Robert Fyfe.
William Cuthil.
Alexander Fulton.
Andrew Glass.
Duncan Donald.
Thomas Penman.
Robert White.
William Sorely.
William Law.
William M'Leish.
James Wright.
David Westwood.
Robert Russell.
Andrew Roy.
John Archibald.
Andrew Henderson.
Andrew Hutcheson.
Peter Dudgeon.
Robert Bean.
Benjamin Taylor.
James Scotland.
John Mercer.
John Smith.
Thomas Baillie.
Alexander M'Gregor.
Thomas Scotland.
James Denman.

'*Signed*—
   William Penman.
   James Taylor.
   Andrew Main.

'*Signed*—
   James Law.
   James Guild.
   Adam Brand.'

After those meetings were held the heritors employed counsel, and took steps to oppose Mr. Watson's plan in Chancery; and thus commenced the Chancery suit which continued for such a long series of years.

Four years after those meetings the inhabitants of Dollar were as much in the dark as ever as to when the parish was to reap the benefit of the legacy; and, getting very impatient at the silence maintained by Mr. Watson and the session, a petition was drawn up and presented to them, signed by fifty-nine names; and another meeting took place in the church on the 16th of June 1812, with the view of meeting the minister and session, and hearing what they had to say in regard to it. None of them, however, having put in an appearance, the meeting appointed the following committee to wait on Mr. Watson in the manse, viz. John Burns, David Smitton, Henry Murray, William M'Leish, Daniel M'Gregor, Andrew Paton, Robert Kirk, James Lawson, Andrew Sharp, Robert Malcolm, and Andrew Mallach. They accordingly waited on him in the manse, and, in the course of a long interview, learned from him that he was determined that his scheme, and his alone, would be adopted, and told them that unless the parish agreed to it, they would never get the legacy. He wanted them to call another meeting of the inhabitants, and get them persuaded to adopt his views, and added: 'Although all the parish should leave me, and the session should leave me, who have acted along with me in the business, yet I stand alone for the poor of the parish;' which meant, of course, for having a poor-house or hospital built, although he knew that this was so generally condemned.

After dragging on for other three long years, the heritors (who were, unfortunately, not trustees under M'Nab's will) were just on the point of losing their suit in Chancery, when, fortunately for Dollar, Mr. Watson died, which put a stop to the proceedings for a time; and Dr. Mylne being appointed his successor, he at once took steps to get the management of the fund transferred from the English Court of Chancery to the proper parties under the will—M'Nab's trustees—to be under the control of the Court of Session in Scotland, and, after nearly two years, succeeded in accomplishing his object. The announcement of Lord Eldon's (the Lord Chancellor) order to this effect, is recorded in the minutes of session on the 26th of June 1818. With the sixteen years' accumulations of interest that had accrued since the death of the testator in 1802, the legacy had now amounted to the handsome sum of £74,000.

BUILDING OF DOLLAR ACADEMY COMMENCED IN 1818.

Dr. Mylne being at one with the heritors and inhabitants of Dollar as to how the money should be applied, it was decided at once to have an educational seminary; and in 1818 the building of Dollar Academy was commenced.

Mr. M'Arbrea's declaration on oath, in 1808, before William Haig, Esq., of Dollarfield, J.P., that, in the conversation he had with Mr. M'Nab when he visited Dollar in 1799, he never mentioned an hospital for the support of the poor, but that the legacy that was to be left was to be for the education of the parish, would have great weight with Dr. Mylne in enabling him to make up his mind on the subject.

Could the worthy donor now return, and see the fine building which his noble generosity was the means of rearing, and learn all the good that had been done in Dollar in the way of education for the last sixty years, not only to the natives of it, but to young men from every part of the world, he would have no reason to regret the decision he came to, or find fault with the admirable way in which the people of Dollar had carried out his wishes.

Dr. Mylne having played such an important part in getting M'Nab's legacy applied to the purpose for which the donor solely intended it, it may not be uninteresting here to give Mr. Tait's letter, appointing him as the Rev. Mr. Watson's successor to the church of Dollar. Mr. Watson (who had been for twenty-three years minister of the parish) died 16th December 1815, and the inhabitants were very anxious to get, as his successor, a Mr. Peter Brydie (afterwards minister of Fossoway), who had for some time been acting as his assistant. With this object in view, a petition in his favour was drawn up for presentation to the patron, Craufurd Tait, Esq., of Harviestoun (the Archbishop of Canterbury's father), and intimation of this had been made to Mr. Tait by letter by my grandfather, James Gibson, one of the elders. This letter brought an answer from Mr. Tait, which I here give a copy of in full.

'EDINBURGH, 20*th Dec.* 1815.

'DEAR SIR,—I have just now received your letter dated the 18th current, mentioning that Mr. Moore, of Lecropt, had assisted the parishioners of Dollar in drawing up a petition to me, for presenting to the Church of Dollar Mr.

Peter Brydie, who has been for some short time past assisting Mr. Watson, the late minister, and that you understand Mr. Brydie would be agreeable to the parish. I have no doubt of Mr. Brydie being a very good man, and it is a great mark of his ability having interested the parish so much in his favour upon so short an acquaintance. But there is a very excellent man, with whom I and all my family have been most intimately acquainted now for more than these twelve years, and I have granted a presentation of the Church of Dollar in his favour. He is a religious and good man, of kind and obliging manners, and of great knowledge and learning; and I am sure I do not venture too far, when I pledge myself that you and the other elders, and all the parish, will, upon experience, find him to be a good minister and a kind friend. His name is Mr. Andrew Mylne, and it is probable that you and many people in the parish have seen him, as he has been frequently at different times living with me and my family at Harviestoun. Many patrons keep the parish vacant for nearly six months; but I am sure that you and the elders will approve of my having granted the presentation without delay, since I know so thoroughly the worth and qualities of Mr. Mylne. —I am, with great regard, dear sir, yours faithfully,

'CRAUFURD TAIT.

'Mr. Gibson, merchant, Dollar.'

Notwithstanding the good account of Mr. Mylne (then pronounced 'Mill') contained in Mr. Tait's letter, there somehow came to Dollar a report about him, that as a teacher in Edinburgh he was considered rather severe in his discipline; and to distinguish him from another Mr. Mylne, also a teacher there, the good folks of Edinburgh 'dubbed' our worthy Doctor 'The Threshing Mill.' Be this as it may, he had no opportunity of using the tawse in Dollar; but from our after experience of him, I would be inclined to think there was some truth in the story.

As soon as it was finally resolved on having an educational seminary, and the building of the Academy was commenced, a few teachers were at once appointed; and until the Academy was finished, they taught in the 'Big Toll-house.'

Mr. James Walker, from Dunbar, was appointed English master; Mr. Peter Steven, for writing and arithmetic; Mr. William Tennant, for Latin, Greek, and Hebrew; Mr. De-Joux (pronounced by the Dollar folks De-Zhue) and his son, for French; and, shortly after the Academy was opened, Mr. Bell was appointed for mathematics. These formed the teaching staff of Dollar Academy for many years. Mr. Steven didn't come for a few months after Mr. Walker, and Mr. George Taylor, of the old town, who lived opposite my father's house, was temporarily appointed to teach writing and arithmetic, and filled the situation very satisfactorily till the permanent teacher came. After a time, Mr. Patrick Gibson was appointed the first drawing-master in the Academy; and, on Mr. Bell resigning the situation of mathematical teacher, Mr. Thomas Mathieson was appointed to succeed him. Mr. Mathieson died on the 13th of June 1833, at the early age of twenty-nine. Mr. David Gray succeeded Mr. Mathieson, and Mr. Gibson's successor in the drawing class was Mr. Patrick Syme.

Mr. Walker's first residence, when he came to Dollar, was Easter Dollarbeg. Mr. De-Joux lived in Dollar Bank. This Frenchman, who had travelled, thought the Devon Valley so like the Vale of Tempē, that he styled his place of residence Tempē Bank; and the vale below, the Vale of Tempē; and in my young days his beautifully-situated residence was regularly called Tempē Bank.

DOLLAR INSTITUTION.
DOLLAR.

W.Banks & Son, Edin.

AN OLD DAME'S SCHOOL.

It must not be thought that Dollar, previous to the inauguration of its now celebrated Academy, was entirely without the means of education; for, in addition to the parish school, it was possessed of a rather famous educational establishment I used to hear a good deal about in my young days, but which had ceased to exist long before my time, and to which I will now refer; this was 'Muckle Jean's School.'

Previous to the fine block of buildings, styled Brooklynn, being built (to the north side of the Academy garden), there stood on the same site three one-storied thatched houses, named Lowburn, the western one of which, during the end of last century and beginning of the present, was the domicile and seminary of this worthy old dame. Her name was Jean Christie; and, to distinguish her from another of the same name, but of smaller stature, she was styled 'Muckle Jean.'

Jean, it seems, didn't approve of a little pair of tawse for keeping order in her school, but used a long wand, with which she could reach the farthest-away scholar without the trouble of rising; and this wand got to be spoken of as a standard of measurement among her scholars—' as long as Muckle Jean's wand ' being a common expression used about anything that was considered very long.

We can easily imagine that Jean was not only innocent of having any knowledge of the classics, but that her acquaintance with the King's English would be but very imperfect; and when any very tough word was reached, that was not only beyond the comprehension of her scholars, but of Jean herself, she got over the difficulty by telling them to 'hip it, daughtie' (pass it over).

I have got these particulars about 'Muckle Jean' from a worthy old friend of mine, who, when a child, lived next door to her.

In connection with Mr. M'Arbrea, the parish teacher (to whom I have already referred), this same old friend of mine told me a rather amusing story about the very reprehensible practice of giving every one a nickname in those days, and which, I am sorry to say, is still too common amongst boys at the present time.

The sexton having died, the Rev. Mr. Watson asked a weaver named John M'Donald to accept of the berth; but John didn't see how he could make his 'daily bread' at it, and wouldn't, therefore, accept of the post. From that time forward John was dubbed 'Daily Bread;' and not only did he get this name, but it descended to his family. One of his sons, Robert— a silly sort of a lad—was much annoyed one day by his schoolfellows shouting 'Daily Bread' to him; when, exasperated beyond measure, he rushed in to Mr. M'Arbrea, and complained bitterly to him about the boys calling him names. Sympathizing with the poor afflicted lad, and wishing to put a stop to this very bad practice, Mr. M'Arbrea asked him who were the guilty parties, when Robert amusingly replied, 'It was Davie Halley, the "Bulldoug," and the "Sparrow."' The spell was broken at once, and poor Bob was found just as guilty as the rest.

This Davie Halley I remember as a pretty old man, with a large family, who carried on a cooperage at the head of Craigie's Brae, and went always by the name of 'Cooper Halley.'

CHAPTER IV.

MEAL MILL AND BIG WHEEL BELOW CASTLE CAMPBELL WOOD.

ABOUT seventy years ago there stood, a little below the foot of Castle Campbell Wood, on the east side of the burn, a dwelling-house and meal mill, which were occupied by a Mr. William M'Leish (father of the Rev. John M'Leish, Free Church minister of Methven). I have no recollection of the mill, but remember the dwelling-house very well, and it was in it that the Rev. John M'Leish was born. The course of the old lade for this mill can still be distinctly traced up to near the Black Linn. At a little distance below the mill (and right above the stream, which runs from the Bog Well), Mr. Tait erected a very large wheel (some 30 feet high), which in my young days was a very conspicuous object in the landscape. Why he put it there, no one seems now to know ; but he had had it previously erected on Kelly Burn, with the view of pumping the water from the various coal-pits around. Mr. M'Whannel, however, the proprietor of Westertown, objected to the scheme, and raised an action in the Court of Session against Mr. Tait, to prohibit its being used ; and, being successful in the suit, the wheel had to be removed, and Mr. Tait re-erected it, as already stated, a little way below the meal mill. He must have had some object in view in putting it there, but had evidently

changed his mind regarding it, as I believe he only
saw it go round once. It rested on a strongly-built,
raised-up arc, and must have cost a large sum of money
to put it there. It was broken up and removed in the
year 1836, and not a vestige of it now remains.

Mr. Tait seems to have contemplated making Dollar
an important manufacturing town, and, with this object
in view, had the ground surveyed from the Bank Burn
down to the foot of Dollar Banks, and got plans prepared (which are still in existence) of the number of
waterfalls that might be made available for a series of
mills. Fortunately, however, for Dollar (as a place of
education) he had rather an extravagant idea of the
value of water power, and none of the falls were
ever taken off; and hence this scheme fell to the
ground.

Another instance of the public spirit of the worthy
proprietor of Harviestoun, and his wish to benefit
Dollar, was the erection of a very large building, nearly
opposite the old Toll-house, which he intended for an
hotel; but it was never occupied as such. Being under
the impression that Dollar would very rapidly increase
after the opening of the Academy, he built this hotel
in anticipation of its requirements, but it unfortunately
turned out a very bad speculation, as it never found a
tenant. A stray room or two of it was now and again
let to separate families, but the bulk of it continued
unoccupied; and, finally, it was removed to make room
for Freshfield Villas, which now occupy its site. It
went always by the name of the ' Big Toll-house,'
and was a very conspicuous object on entering Dollar.
It was on the side of this building that the hustings
were erected, on nomination days, for members of
Parliament; and here it was that the Tory candidates

used to get every species of abuse hurled at them—
Dollar being then, as now, ' Liberal ' to the core.

There was one public undertaking carried out through
the influence of Mr. Tait, and the extra cost of which
was, I understand, borne by him, that the inhabitants
of the locality are still enjoying the pleasure of,—and
that was the making of the new turnpike road between
Dollar and Tillicoultry, in its winding, picturesque
form, instead of (as between Alva and Tillicoultry) in
an almost straight line. This road has added very
much to the beauty of the district, and a lovelier drive
than between Dollar and Tillicoultry, through Harviestoun estate, with the fine range of the Ochil Hills rising
abruptly, and to a great height, in the immediate back-
ground, could not be found anywhere. Harviestoun
Castle itself is a noble building, and the situation in
which it stands is one of the finest, perhaps, in
Scotland. The clear-winding Devon, passing through
the grounds, adds greatly to the beauty of the magnificent scenery. It was while on a visit to the Tait
family at Harviestoun Castle that Burns wrote the
following verse, regarding Miss Charlotte Hamilton, a
visitor at the time along with himself :—

' How pleasant the banks of the clear-winding Devon,
  With green-spreading bushes, and flowers blooming fair,
But the bonniest flower on the banks of the Devon
  Was once a sweet bud on the braes of the Ayr.'

When referring to the poet Burns, it may not be out
of place here, in passing, to give a few lines I saw
somewhere, written on the anniversary of the poet's
birth. He was born on the 25th of January 1759,
and died on July 22nd 1796, aged only thirty-seven
years and six months.

'Sax score o' years and three the nicht,
Ha'e skelpit on wi' a' their micht,
Since Scotland's Poet saw the licht,
    'Mid storms and tears :
They ne'er tak time their feet tae dicht—
    Thae madcap years.'

BIRD'S-EYE VIEW OF THE DEVON VALLEY AND ARCHBISHOP OF CANTERBURY PEAK.

To any one who wishes to see the lovely valley of the Devon in all its beauty, let him take a bird's-eye view of it, as I did this summer, and he will be amply rewarded for his trouble. Starting from Dollar one fine evening, I went up to the top of Dollarbank Hill, and then walked straight along to Tillicoultry on the top of the front hills; and the grandeur of the scene was beyond anything I had ever conceived of, and I wondered very much I had been so long in witnessing it. Standing on the top of one of the front peaks, a little to the east of Harviestoun Castle (which, by the way, I will now take the liberty of naming the Archbishop of Canterbury Peak, from his father's beautiful mansion below being so long the home of his youth), the fine building seems almost at your feet; and the beautifully - wooded grounds of the estate, with the clear-winding Devon—like a streak of silver—meandering through them, forms one of the finest panoramas, I believe, that can be seen anywhere in Britain. The hills rise so abruptly, you have quite the feeling of looking down on the lovely scene from a tower of at least a thousand feet high. Then the view from this peak (which stands out in front of the range) in the distance is very fine, embracing, as it does, the towns of Stirling, Alloa, Clackmannan, Saline, Menstrie, Alva,

ABBEY CRAIG & WINDINGS OF THE FORTH.
From Stirling Castle.

Drawn & Engd by W Banks & Son Edin

Tillicoultry, Dollar, Kinross, with the river Forth, Loch Leven, and all the finely-wooded country for thirty miles around.

The burn that passes Mr. Miller's lodge, and which divides Tillicoultry parish from that of Dollar, rises behind this peak, and passes close to the east side of it. The peak, therefore, is in Tillicoultry parish, and at the very eastern extremity of it.

A few years ago I walked from Tillicoultry to Dollar —by way of Helen's Muir, and over the top of the King's Seat (the second highest hill of the Ochils), and the view from the latter is very extensive and grand ; but for real beauty and loveliness, the lower front peaks of the range are much to be preferred.

TAIT'S TOMB.

Although Harviestoun estate has long since passed out of the hands of the Tait family, there is one small sacred spot that still belongs to them—the family burying-place—situated about half-way between Dollar and Tillicoultry, and close to the Devon. It was enclosed with a high wall by the late Mr. Tait ; and in it he and a number of his family are buried, including our late worthy sheriff—John Tait, Esq.—and his wife.

This burying-ground, as is well known, is called Tait's Tomb, and in dark nights was an object of great terror (and will still be, I believe) to the young folks, and very few could summon up courage to pass it. It was not only because of stories about ghosts in connection with it (that we used to hear so much of in my young days) that made us afraid, but because of its being situated in a densely-wooded thicket, and even in ordinary dark nights is extremely dark. From a tombstone in this burying-ground, I find that Craufurd Tait was not the first of the Tait family who was proprietor of Harviestoun estate (as I had always understood), but that his father, John Tait, had been in possession of it before him. This stone was erected by his grandsons, and part of the inscription on it is as follows :—

In memory of
JOHN TAIT, Esqr. of Harviestoun,
and of Cumloden in Argyleshire,
Writer to the Signet.
Born in 1727.   Died in 1800.

Craufurd Tait (son of the above, to whom I have so often referred) died in May 1832, aged sixty-seven. On the stone to his memory the following eulogium is recorded : ' His taste adorned this lovely valley, in the bosom of which he lies. His genius—in advance of the age in which he lived—originated, in a great measure, the improvement of the district, and pointed the way to much throughout the country destined to be accomplished by a future generation.'

Mrs. Craufurd Tait died 3rd January 1814.

From the inscription on the stone erected to the memory of our late worthy sheriff, I find he had acted for the long period of forty-four years in that capacity. It is as follows :—

In memory of
JOHN TAIT, Esq.,
Eldest son of Craufurd Tait,
And for 36 years Sheriff of Clackmannan and Kinross,
And 8 years Sheriff of Perth.
Born 11th February 1796.   Died 22nd May 1877.

Mrs. Sheriff Tait died 29th January 1845, so that

the sheriff had been a widower for the long period of thirty-two years.

The deaths of other members of the family are recorded, but it is not quite clear whether they are buried there or not.

One of the memorial stones records the fact that this burying-ground was ' consecrated ' by Archibald Campbell Tait, Archbishop of Canterbury (then Bishop of London), in 1862. On it is the following inscription, followed by some suitable verses from the Bible : ' He desires here, amongst the graves of his kindred, to commemorate his wife, Catherine Tait, and his son, the Rev. Craufurd Tait, M.A., who were both buried at Addington in 1878. Also his five daughters, buried at Stanwix, near Carlisle, in 1756.'

I recollect well the deep sympathy felt for the Archbishop (then Dean of Carlisle) throughout the length and breadth of the land, when the overwhelming bereavement came upon him, in the death of five of his daughters at one time, from that terrible disease—scarlet fever; and how much, it was said, the highest lady in the land—our worthy Queen—sympathized with him under the unparalleled blow.

OLD BUILDINGS IN DOLLAR.

The second wool mill of Dollar was built by Mr. William Drysdale, of Alva, who carried it on for a very long time ; and after his death, his son Robert continued in it for a great many years. The water for the wheel of this mill was brought, in a raised-up wooden trough, from the weir previously mentioned, and stood right above where the Castle walk now is. When not required for the wheel, the water was discharged into the burn by a large spout immediately behind the mill. A long row of stenters, for drying their goods, stood on the opposite side of the burn, to the north of Cissy and Annie Sinclair's garden.

After Mr. Robert Drysdale's death, Mr. Peter Stalker bought this mill, and afterwards sold it to Sir Andrew Orr; and it is now the property of his brother, Mr. James Orr. It has now been turned into a comfortable hall for religious meetings, and must be a great acquisition to the old town of Dollar.

Immediately below the upper bridge, on the east side of the burn, there was a long row of one-storied houses in those days, with two houses at the upper end, facing the north (many of the inhabitants of which I remember well), but of which not the slightest vestige now remains.

The next two-storied house to these—nearer the old town—was Mrs. Burns' house (the first Mrs. Peter Stalker's mother), and whose husband was one of the original partners of the first wool mill. I might thus go over almost every house in Dollar (the inhabitants of which were nearly all known to me), but will only refer to a few who were in any way in a public position, and to those with whom we came more immediately in contact, and whose friendship and intercourse we enjoyed.

Below the old church the parish schoolhouse stood, as at present; two one-storied houses opposite Mr. Robertson's, and three or four one-storied houses, named the Kirk Style (where the present Established Church now is), were all the houses on the east side of the burn below the middle bridge; while those houses above this bridge have all been recently built. With the exception of a few houses where the post-office now is, and on the Rack Mill and Lower Mains roads, there were no houses to the south of Bridge Street, and only one between the Station Road and the Big Toll-house. The introduction of the railway, however, in 1869, gave quite an impetus to the prosperity of Dollar, and there is now a good-sized town between Bridge Street and the railway, while beautiful villas have sprung up in all directions.

The Upper Mains has since those days got, in addition to the gasworks, one or two new houses ; but the old ones (including Laird Izat's and the Upper Mains House) remain as of yore. The latter, however, instead of being almost hid from view by a dense shrubbery, is now quite exposed, and surrounded by public roads on all sides. The pillars of the entrance gate alone now remain to show where the approach to the house was.

At the entrance to the road to Gateside, on the right-hand side, the ruins of a house still remain, that was as well known to all the children of Dollar as any house in it ; and many a spare penny found its way there, the decent old body who lived in it (Kirsty Mitchell) being quite famous as a maker of ' black man,' and did a ' roaring trade ' in it.

About a couple of hundred yards west from Kirsty's house, and on the right-hand side of this road (the old highway to Stirling) going west, the very old house of Gateside stood, which was the principal inn of the village in days of old, but was in my young days the dwelling-house of the farm. This house was to me like a second home, and some of the happiest days of my youth are linked up with it.

No more worthy couple than Mr. and Mrs. Robert

Wright—the heads of the family who lived in it—could be found anywhere, and their home was a model of domestic happiness and bliss.

A very antique bed stood in one of the rooms of this house, in which, it was said, the Duke of Argyle slept on one of his visits to Dollar—very probably after the destruction of his castle by the Duke of Montrose. The stables in connection with it alone now remain, at the west end of which it stood.

Being the principal companions of my youth, I will here give the names of this family: Robert, John, William, Ann, and James.

Robert established an excellent business as a writer in Greenock, but died a good many years ago, leaving his widow (Miss Catherine Kirk, of Park House, Dollar) and a numerous family to mourn his early death. The business is being successfully carried on by some members of his family.

John has been the much-respected minister of the Free Church of Kinross for nearly forty years, having been inducted to this charge shortly after the Disruption.

William commenced business as a writer in Edinburgh, but died when quite a young man, leaving a widow and two or three of a family. He was 'best man' at my marriage.

Ann and James are both married, and comfortably settled in the neighbourhood of Kirkintilloch, where their mother lived for a great many years. She died only last year, being close on a hundred years old; while her husband died about thirty years ago, in Dollar. Mrs. Wright was a sister of Mr. Gentle, so long parish teacher of Fossoway. Of this family, therefore, which was so well known and so much respected for a very long period in Dollar, there is not one of them now remaining in it.

A brewery was carried on at one time at Gateside, but had ceased operations just before my day. I remember well, however, of the building, and of the water running into it, from the well above, for the brewing operations. It stood at right angles to the road, the north end of it being close to where the present dwelling-house now is. It was carried on by old Mr. Wright's father, and it would be from him that the bit of tableland above Gateside got the name of 'The Brewer's Knowe.'

The road from the brewery into Dollar went by the name of the 'Nappy Gate,' from the folks, I suppose, getting rather 'nappy' or 'hearty,' after paying a visit to the brewery.

One of the stipulations, tradition says, in the charter of the land in connection with this old brewery, and on the fulfilment of which alone, it is said, it could be retained, was, that when the king passed, the brewer should be able to present him with five gallons of old brewed ale, five gallons of new, and five from what was in process of brewing.

'OLD CRAIGIE'——DAYS OF THE CORN LAWS.

Sir Henry Wardlaw, Bart.'s, maternal great-grandfather—Mr. Guild, of Craiginnan hill farm—was the last one who lived in the house up at the hill (this hill is frequently called 'The White Wisp,' and 'The Saddle Hill'), and after leaving it he took up his residence in Dollar. He went always by the name of 'Old Craigie' (from Craiginnan); and the steep brae in the north street

F

of the old town where he lived got the name of ' Craigie's
Brae.' His house was situated at the foot of the steepest
part of it. He had passed away before my day, but he
used to be often referred to in my young days. That he
was in the farm in 1799, I have learned on undoubted
authority, but in what year he left it I have not been
able to find out. In that year (long remembered in
these islands as the year of ' the great dearth ') Mrs.
Guild had been fortunate in having had a good stock of
meal laid in, and was very kind to the inhabitants of
Dollar; for as long as her stock lasted, she kindly gave
a supply to all who applied for it; and many were the
applicants she had from the village. Mr. James
Christie's father used to tell them of his going up to
Craiginnan, when a little boy, along with the rest, for a
supply of meal.

In our days of free trade, and when we have the
world for our granary, we can scarcely form any con-
ception of the great straits the people were put to in
those days, and the state of semi-starvation the greater
portion of them were often reduced to; but when it is
stated that the hazel nuts (which were plentiful that
year) were pounded into a sort of meal, and baked into
cakes, and were largely resorted to by the people, some
idea of the dreadful state of matters may be formed.
And yet this is a state of things that might have existed
at the present day if our Tory legislators had had their
will; but thanks to Cobden and Bright, and the noble
band of coadjutors of the Anti-Corn Law League, who
so stirred up the whole country to the crying iniquity
of the Corn Laws, that our legislators were compelled to
abolish them. (I had the pleasure of hearing Messrs.
Cobden and Bright in the City Hall of Glasgow when on
their first grand tour of agitation throughout the country.)

One of Mr. Guild's shepherds, John Christie, had been much in advance of his day (and, indeed, of our own day), for he was possessed of a library of nearly 400 volumes, in various departments of literature; which shows him to have been a man of a very literary turn of mind, and 'one among a thousand.' Few, indeed, in much higher walks of life, can at the present time boast of such a library. When we think, too, of the much greater cost of books in those days than now, the acquisition of such a library by a humble shepherd seems all the more astonishing. What a pity such a unique collection of books had not been preserved; but such, it seems, had not been the case, for at John's death they were sold by auction at the end of the old town bridge, and are scattered abroad, no one knows where. He was born in 1712, and baptized on the 12th of October.

Mr. James Wardlaw, ironmonger (descended from the Wardlaws of Pitreavie, and cousin of the present Baronet), is one of the very few old natives of Dollar who are left in it, and was one of my most intimate school companions. His brother Alexander succeeded to my father's business when he died, in 1846, and carried it on successfully for a long period.

There was one most energetic, pushing business lady in the old town, to whom, and her husband and family, I will now briefly refer—Mrs. Tod (sister of Mr. Mein, of Mein's Hotel, Trongate, Glasgow, one of the great hotels of the city in the 'coaching days'). She carried on a most extensive baking business, and supplied the country for miles around with bread—her carts going regularly as far as Oakley, Saline, etc. Mr. David Tod, her husband, was of a quiet, retiring disposition, and superintended some small farming operations which they carried on as well. They had only two of a family, George and Agnes, who were amongst the most cherished companions, of my youth ; but who were both cut off at an early age, and when full of promise. Agnes died on 21st September 1844, aged twenty-two, and there was one sadly torn heart amongst the teachers of Dollar Academy when she was laid in her grave.

Mr. Tod died on the 14th of January 1845. After his death Mrs. Tod retired from business, and lived for some years in the new town. She died on the 7th of June 1850. George (a very excellent young man) was in a writer's office in Edinburgh, and was cut off at the early age of thirty, on the 6th of December 1852. Four little shrubs mark the spot where they now lie, near the north-east corner of the old churchyard.

Their premises in the old town now go by the name of ' The Lorne Tavern.'

CHAPTER V.

I WILL now give the names of the teachers in the Academy when I was at school.

Mr. James Walker, English teacher; Mr. Charles M'Intosh, Mr. Walker's assistant; Mr. Peter Steven, writing and arithmetic; Mr. Power, Mr. Steven's assistant; Mr. William Tennant (afterwards Professor in St. Andrews, and Author of *Anster Fair*), Latin, Greek, and Hebrew; Mr. Balfour, Mr. Tennant's assistant; Mr. David Gray (afterwards Professor in Aberdeen), mathematics; Mr. Thomas Martin, teacher of geography, and librarian to the Institution ; Mr. Patrick Syme, drawing ; Mr. Gerlach, French, German, etc. ; Mrs. Brydie, sewing mistress ; Miss Spittal, Mrs. Brydie's assistant; Mr. Thomas Russell, infant teacher; Mr. Gibson (a very worthy man), janitor.

THE OLD CHURCH OF DOLLAR—REV. DR. MYLNE, ETC.

About the year 1841 the old Established Church ceased to be used as a place of worship, the present handsome church being then erected. The old church (we learn from the Statistical Account of Scotland) was rebuilt in the year 1775, and was considered a very

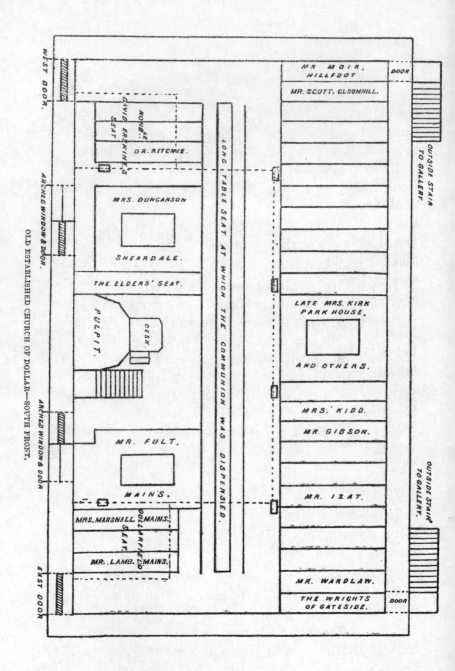

OLD ESTABLISHED CHURCH OF DOLLAR.—SOUTH FRONT.

neat little church. I have a distinct recollection of this
old building, in which the late Dr. Mylne for upwards
of twenty-five years preached; and give herewith a
rough sketch of its internal arrangements—the front of
the gallery, and two of the seats in it, being in dotted
lines. I have also given a few of the names of those
to whom the seats belonged.

Robert Forrester was precentor in the old church
from as far back as I can recollect, till its close; and
John Christie was beadle. There was a square seat in
the front of the west gallery, where the Honourable
David Erskine, of Broomrig (now Mr. Leishman's house),
and his family sat; while the corresponding seat in the
east gallery was occupied by Mr. Haig's family of
Dollarfield.

Mr. Erskine (the grandfather of the present Earl of
Mar and Kellie) was very short of stature, and blind;
but Mrs. Erskine was a tall, fine-looking lady, and their
family were generally tall. Charles attended Dollar
Academy for a number of years; but Colonel Erskine,
his eldest brother (afterwards Earl of Mar and Kellie),
never resided in Dollar.

The communion was observed in those days only
once a year, and some folks seemed to think that by
'showing face' in the church on those occasions, and
attending on all the 'preaching days' (as they were
called)—the Fast-day, Saturday, and Monday—they
were giving quite enough attention to the concerns of
eternity. They 'prepared' themselves for the sacrament, and, after it was past, thought no more, apparently, about these things, till next year again, as they
were never seen in church till the next communion
season. I recollect well of some such who sat near our
seat in the low church, on whom we could thus calcu-

late of being sure to see in church at least once a year. On those sacramental occasions a tent was generally erected in the churchyard, and preaching was carried on in it and in the church at the same time. People went long distances to attend sacraments, and great gatherings were often to be seen around the tents. The Fast-day was looked upon as of quite as solemn a nature as the Sabbath, and for any one to be seen doing any kind of work on that day, was sufficient to stamp him at once ' as a regular heathen,' and quite a proper subject to be taken before the session. (The old session records of Tillicoultry can tell some most amusing stories in regard to this; and very probably those of Dollar, and most other places in Scotland, can do the same. A man was taken before the session in Tillicoultry for putting his horse into his cart on the Fast-day, and pleaded as his excuse that he quite forgot it was the Fast-day.

About the year 1640, when Mr. Carmichael was minister of Markinch, great stress seems to have been laid on special days of fasting, and almost every month the people were called upon 'to bewaill their own sinnes, and ye sinnes of ye land;' and so sacred were those days considered, that the people were forbidden to ' think their own thoughts, or do their own deeds' upon them. From the session records of this parish, I give the following extracts as a specimen of the reasons given for those frequent days of fasting :—

'6*th January* 1644.—Collected by David Dalrymple, and James Wilsone. . . . (being ane preperation to an fast), for ye causes following: Imprimo, To bewaill our own sinnes, and ye sinnes of ye land. 2. That God would grant ane end to ye distractions of England and distractions of Ireland. 3. That He would grant ane

prosperous success to ye Parliament of England and Con-
vention of Divines mett ther, and our Comnnissioners
present with them. 4. That God would grant an prosperous success to our armie intending to goe to England.'

' *27th October* 1644.—This day was appointed to be ane
day of humiliatione. . . . We have great reason to be
humbled in a solemne manner by fasting and prayer,
becaus we see ye anger of God is kindled against us in
ane extraordinary way, as is evidently seen and felt—
1. By slow progress of ye much-wished wark of refor-
matione. 2. Bye long continuance of thois bloodie and
unnatural warres within this kingdom. 3. By this un-
happie division betwixt the king and his subjects,
fomented by ye popishe and prelaticall faction with their
adherents and malignantis. 4. By ye breach alreadie
maid by a contemptible crew, naked and unarmed, upon
our dear brethren in Stratherne, Fyffe, Aberdene, and
other parts in ye north, with effusion of much Christian
blood, and spoyling of goodis, whereby many honest
women are made desolat widowis, many children father-
less, and whole families brought to extreme povertie. We
are turned back in ye day off battell, and fled as ye
Israelites before Ai, so we fled before a base, unarmed,
and inconsiderable enemie.'

' *21st September* 1645.—The whilk day was ane thanks-
giving for the happie victorie obtained by Lievtenant-
Generall David Leslie against James Grahame, sometyme
Earl of Montross, and his rebellis at Philip-Haugh, neir
Jedburch, upon ye 13th of September 1645.'

When referring to the observance of Fast-days—special
and sacramental—in days of old, it may not be out of
place here to give an amusing incident, showing the rigidly
strict way the Sabbath was kept in some houses not
long ago. A young gentleman of our own neighbour-
bood paid a visit, when a little boy, to the manse on a
Sabbath-day, and to his great horror the minister's dog
—a brisk little frisky thing—was romping about through

the house, enjoying itself, as dogs will do, even on the Sabbath-day, when the question was at once asked by my ' young hopeful,' ' Why does yer dog play on the Sabbath-day ? ' to which the minister's lady replied, ' Oh, you know, James, the dog doesn't know any better.' ' A-weel (says Jamie) if it wis in oor hoose it wid be gard ken ' (made to know).

Dr. Mylne didn't trouble himself much about composing sermons ; for having, apparently, a good stock when he came to Dollar, he made them ' stand him in good stead ' during the whole of his sojourn there. So much was this the case, that I think nearly the whole of his congregation would be able to repeat the most of them from end to end. I recollect well of an amusing story in connection with this. A worthy old lady from Auchterarder (Mrs. Dewar, a cousin of my father's) was paying us a visit, and heard the Doctor lecture on a favourite theme of his, ' The Ten Virgins.' Coming back some ten years afterwards, the Doctor again lectured on the same subject, and very naturally and simply the good old lady asked, ' Does Dr. Mylne always preach on " The Ten Virgins " ? '

The worthy Doctor seemed to begin at the top of his pile of sermons, and went regularly down to the bottom ; and when that was reached, turned them upside down, and repeated the process over again ; and so on, year after year, till the end of his days.

AN OLD LADY'S OPINION OF WHAT CONSTITUTED ' A CHRISTIAN.'

A good story is told of two worthy old dames of Dollar, one of whom I remember well, which shows the

idea that some folks had in those days of what constituted ' *a Christian.*' The worthy ladies were gossiping
one day on the character of one of their neighbours (a
well-known man in Dollar), and took opposite views as
to his being ' a Christian ; ' when one of them ' clinched '
the argument by exclaiming, ' Him a Christian ! na, na,
he's no that, for he never pits siller in the plate.'
(This is a good hint to the late Dr. William Anderson's
' 10*d. to the score*' sort.)

For a number of years after Dollar Academy was
commenced, the kirk-session was often composed of a
very few members, and for some time previous to the
year 1826, of only two, viz. Robert Smith, a shoemaker, and a James Christie, who were seldom consulted by Dr. Mylne about the affairs of the Institution; so that during that time he was virtually the
sole ruler in everything connected with it, and, as
almost invariably happens when too much power is left
in the hands of one man, he ruled with a very high
hand. He expelled scholars for the most trivial offences,
and issued some very arbitrary decrees. As a specimen
of the latter, I subjoin the following correspondence,
which will explain itself :—

From MR. M'KELVIE to DR. MYLNE.

'DOLLAR, 24*th July* 1826.

' REV. SIR,—Having heard some surmises that it is
your intention, after the coming vacation, to prevent
persons keeping boarders in Dollar from engaging young
men of the Secession Church as tutors, and being unable
to learn the truth of these surmises, I have taken the
liberty of writing you, to request that you would make
me aware, by letter or otherwise, if such really be your
intention. Your doing so will confer a favour, as it will

enable me to make such arrangements as your determination may require.

'I have been informed that you have come to the above resolution in consequence of a report having reached you that the Stirling Secession Presbytery hesitated to grant Mr. Skinner licence, because he attended on your ministry. I was present when Mr. S. was licensed, and think it a duty I owe to that gentleman, and to the Presbytery, to say that such a subject was never once alluded to.—I am, etc.,

'W. M'KELVIE.'

[This Mr. M'Kelvie (afterwards Dr. M'Kelvie) was the much-esteemed minister of Balgeddie for thirty-four years (from 1829 till 1863), and author of the *Annals and Statistics of the U. P. Church;* and of *The Life and Vindication of Michael Bruce.*]

DR. MYLNE'S Answer.

'DR. MYLNE begs to acknowledge the receipt of Mr. M'Kelvie's note, and expresses his regret that, owing to his being from home, and the pressure of some urgent business, it has not been in his power to reply to it sooner.

'It is quite true that the Trustees of M'Nab's Legacy have determined, that after the vacation all persons taking the charge of the pupils attending M'Nab's School must set their pupils the example of attending the Parish Church. It amounts to the same thing whether the absence of the tutors from the Parish Church be the result of their own choice, or an act of obedience to the orders of others.

'As to what actually passed in the Presbytery of the Secession Church, the Trustees of 'M'Nab's Legacy have no right to know, neither is it any concern of theirs; for whatever happened on the occasion alluded to, cannot affect the general question.

'DOLLAR MANSE, 28*th July* 1826.'

On inquiry being made at the Doctor's two elders about the issuing of this order, it was found that they had never been consulted in the matter, and were quite opposed to it; and when taken to task about this, the Doctor frankly confessed that he never thought of consulting them about anything in connection with the Academy; but that he always, nevertheless, issued his mandates in the name of 'the Trustees;' and that, in this instance, he had just acted according to his usual practice.

This state of matters caused much discontent throughout the parish, and finally led to a movement being set on foot to get the Doctor to appoint a number of new elders, to act along with him in the management of the Trust. The first to move in the matter was Captain Pinkerton, who waited on Captain Porteous, to ascertain his views about the existing state of things; and both together called on Dr. Elliot; and all the three were of one opinion, that something must be done at once to prevent the Academy being ruined.

Those three, then, commenced an agitation in Dollar, which, after a number of meetings of the inhabitants had been held, and an extensive correspondence had taken place, finally compelled Dr. Mylne to appoint a number of new elders; and on Sabbath the 12th of November 1826, the following gentlemen were inducted into office:—Messrs. Craufurd Tait of Harviestoun; John Tait (sheriff); William Haig, Dollarfield; James Haig, Dollarfield; William Clark, Dollarbeg; John M'Arthur Moir, Hillfoot; Robert Kirk, Dollar; and William Gibson, Dollar. [Mr. William Gibson (the writer's father) was, after a time, appointed secretary and treasurer, and continued so till his death.]

This large accession to the number of the Trustees

took the responsibility off Dr. Mylne's head to a great extent; and although it did not altogether allay the strong feeling that had been raised up against him by many of his acts, it was a great improvement upon the old *régime.* The new Trustees did not, however, find their new berths 'a bed of roses;' for a feeling had been stirred up amongst a number of the folks that M'Nab's Legacy should have been divided amongst them; and this was carried to such an extent, that an action was actually raised in the Court of Session against the Trustees, concluding for the modest sum of £70,000. This, however, by the energy of Dr. Mylne and his able body of Trustees, was speedily defeated, and the noble Institution, with all its benefits, secured to Dollar. A Mr. George Somerville, of the New Town (who had some legal knowledge), took a very active part in this 'law plea,' and was ever afterwards spoken of in connection with it.

Notwithstanding the assistance of such a large number of Trustees, a good deal of grumbling was still kept up in the parish about the management of the Trust; and, to put an end to this, Dr. Mylne finally resolved to petition Parliament to get a Board of Trustees appointed on a new basis; and an Act was accordingly got in 1847, constituting a new Board, as follows: The parish minister and only four of his session were now to be Trustees, those four to be chosen by the session, and to continue for life. Two members of the Stirling Presbytery, and two representative members for the parishioners of Dollar—chosen every five years—were now to be Trustees; and any gentleman possessed of £200 annual income from heritable property in the county of Clackmannan, and paying taxes in the parish of Dollar, is eligible for being a Trustee.

The Principal of the University of Edinburgh, the Lord-Lieutenant, Vice-Lieutenant, Convener, and Sheriff of the county of Clackmannan, and the patron of the parish of Dollar, are also Trustees.

Dr. Mylne was a man of great talent, and was the author of several educational books of intrinsic value ; amongst others, an excellent English Grammar, an elementary book on Astronomy, questions on the histories of England, of Greece, and of Rome ; and he was also a contributor to the *Encyclopædia Britannica* when it was brought out.

The Doctor was short of stature, very stout, of a ruddy complexion, and wore a dark wig, which made him look younger than he really was. An excellent portrait of him is to be seen in the Trustees' room of the Institution, presented by Mrs. Edmonstone (Mrs. Mylne's residuary legatee), through Mr. Haig of Dollarfield.

From the long intimacy that existed between Sheriff Tait and Dr. Mylne, the sheriff should have been able to form a pretty correct opinion of him ; and in a lecture on ' Dollar,'—delivered by the sheriff in 1867, —he says of him, 'that although he had a quick and irascible temper, he had under it all a kind heart ;' in charity, therefore, to the old Doctor, let us hope the sheriff's estimate of him was correct. He died in 1856, aged eighty-one years, in the forty-first year of his ministry.

My father's burying-ground is right in front of the west door of the old church, and there lie the remains of my Grandfather and Grandmother Gibson, Uncle James, my father and mother, and five of their family— my eldest sister, Jeanie (Mrs. Dalgleish), having been buried in Stirling Cemetery.

The interior of the old church is now, I find, turned into a large tomb. The old Doctor lies right under where the pulpit was, in which he so long preached. Mr. and Mrs. Martin of Springfield are buried under their old seat in the gallery. Mr. Peter Stalker's burying-ground is exactly where the Wrights of Gateside and Mr. Wardlaw's family used to sit. Mr. Brown's is where my father's seat was.

I may here give one or two facts regarding Dollar, as recorded in the Statistical Account of Scotland, written by the Rev. Mr. Watson in the year 1792. The population of Dollar at that time was 510. The poor of the parish were supported by the church-door collections; and, taking the average of a number of years, cost £21 annually. Mr. Watson says, 'There have been no beggars in this parish in the memory of man.' Average number of poor on the roll, 9.

' Mr. John M'Arbrea, the parish schoolmaster, teaches English, Latin, Writing, Arithmetic, etc., and is much respected. His fixed salary is only £100 Scotch, but he draws the interest of 560 merks Scotch of sunk money, besides perquisites as precentor and session-clerk,' etc. He was appointed parish teacher in 1763, and died in March 1820, aged eighty-four years.

In this Statistical Account the Devon is called the Dovan, but I think it must have been about this time its name was changed; for the Rev. Mr. Osborne, in the *first* part of his *Statistical Account of Tillicoultry Parish*, calls it also the *Dovan*, but in the *latter* part the *Devon*. Mr. Watson says that in harvest time sea-trouts of from 2 lbs. to 4 lbs. weight are killed in the Devon; and in the season, salmon from 5 lbs. to 20 lbs. ' About twenty to thirty years ago, salmon were found in Dovan in great plenty; but, from the illegal and murderous manner of killing them with spears, their numbers of late have greatly decreased.'

Three coal-works were being carried on at that time in Dollar parish, two belonging to the Duke of Argyle, and one to Lord Alva. Mr. Watson says, ' Ironstone is also found in different parts of the parish, and said to be of very excellent quality. It is working at present by the Dovan Company, who are now erecting a public work at Sauchie, some miles to the westward, in the parish of Clackmannan.'

' Paterfamilias ' with large families would rejoice to see those grand old days of cheap provisions back again. Butcher meat sold at from 3d. to $4\frac{1}{4}$d. per lb., Dutch weight; a good hen for from 9d. to 1s.; eggs, 3d. to 4d. per dozen; butter, 6d. per lb.; cheese, $3\frac{1}{2}$d. But while the price of provisions would please, the rate of wages, I am afraid, would be decidedly objected to; and, all things considered, we would be ready to think that we are just as well as we are. Wages of women at out-door work, 6d. per day, at harvest time 10d. per day, without provisions; ploughmen, £6 yearly; women servants, £2, 10s. yearly; a mason's wage, 1s. 8d. to 2s. per day; a joiner's, 1s. 6d. to 1s. 8d.; a tailor's, 8d.; a slater's, 2s.

The Academy having been opened in 1820, my father's family all had the advantage of being educated there, under some of the best teachers, perhaps, that have ever been in it.

Mr. Walker, who—as I have already said—was the first English master in the Academy, was a most excellent teacher, and a strict disciplinarian, and continued for a very long time the much-respected master in this department of the Academy. He could give a very effective ' paumie,' and we had a most wholesome dread

G

of his tawse, and endeavoured, of course, to merit their acquaintance as seldom as possible, by having our lessons thoroughly well prepared. He was, at the same time, a most kind and affectionate man, and possessed the affection and esteem of all his pupils.

He was twice married, and had a very large family, ten of whom (two daughters and a son, of the first marriage; and two daughters and five sons, of the second) predeceased him; and his memorial-stone in the old churchyard shows how very heavily he and his partners in life had been bereaved. His widow and Miss Walker only are now resident in Dollar; and only one son, Mr. Andrew, survives of the second marriage.

Miss Walker, James, and Isabella (Mrs. Middleton) were my school companions. William (who was considerably older than I) and James have been long settled in Canada.

Mr. Walker died in 1871, aged eighty-four years.

Mr. Steven was a very worthy man, and one of the best writers, I believe, in Britain. The scholars used to take their prizes to him to get their names written on them, and many books throughout the world —possessed by old pupils of the Academy, from every clime—can still bear testimony to the beauty of his writing. The ornamental 'specimens' (which he pencilled) of the scholars, for exhibition on the examination days, and which were afterwards inked by them, were fine examples of his great gift in ornamental penmanship; and the walls of many a room are still adorned by fine framed specimens of these; but perhaps no finer example of his beautiful work can be seen anywhere than in Dollar old churchyard. When the Academy was building in 1819, one of the masons, named David Millar, was fatally injured, and died shortly afterwards; and his master, Thomas Beattie, the contractor for the work, erected a stone to his memory, near the east side of the old burying-ground, the lettering and ornamental work on which had been designed by Mr. Steven. I was never told so; but on taking a walk through the churchyard one day with my brother, and on coming to this stone, I at once said, 'That's Mr. Steven;' there could be no mistaking it.

He was a most enthusiastic curler, and my father and he had many a night of it on the Academy garden pond, with a lantern at each tee. He died in 1855, aged sixty-four years.

Margaret, his eldest daughter, was married to Mr. Maxton, a civil engineer.

Anne married Mr. Peter Stalker; and Jane was married to Dr. Lindsay.

Miss Clarke (the second Mrs. Steven's sister) was an accomplished musician, and was for a long period the principal music teacher in Dollar.

Mr. Tennant, teacher of Latin, Greek, and Hebrew, lived in Devongrove. He was a most amiable man, and a very learned scholar. He was very lame, and used two crutches, and had a long walk daily to school. Miss Tennant, his sister, who kept house for him, was one of the most amiable creatures that ever lived, and was a great favourite with everybody; and it must have added greatly to her brother's comfort having such a kind and affectionate sister to take charge of his household.

Mr. Thomas Martin, teacher of geography, and librarian to the Academy, built and lived in Springfield, at present owned and occupied by Mrs. Driver and her family. Large additions have been made to it by the present owner.

Mr. Gerlach, the French teacher, was a Swiss, and a very violent-tempered man, and the scholars generally were so much afraid of him that many didn't go to his class at all (myself amongst the rest); and hence, to my great loss now, I never learned French, which I miss very much. I recollect he was very anxious to learn Scotch, and used to talk to the scholars on the road; and when he heard any thoroughly broad Scotch word, would repeat it after them, and ask what it meant.

Mr. Syme, the drawing-master, was a man of great taste, and a most successful teacher. Landscapes and flowers were his forte, and figures and faces were seldom or ever taught by him. I have still some of my attempts at landscapes, in water-colours, when under him.

Mr. Gray, who taught mathematics, was a very talented man, and there was no class in the Academy I enjoyed more than his.

Mrs. Brydie, and Miss Spittal, her assistant, were most efficient teachers in their own department, and were both very much respected by all in Dollar. There were few evening parties of young folks but Miss Spittal formed one of them.

Mr. Thomas Russell (now of Clackmannan), who taught the infant school, was a most admirable teacher of the young. Full of spirit, and abounding in anecdotes, and naturally 'cut out' for the training of a large number of children, it was quite a treat to witness an examination of his young charge. He married the eldest daughter of a well-known and old-established merchant of the New Town—Mr. Charles Lawson.

Mr. Power was a fine-looking young man, and a great favourite in Dollar. Mr. Balfour was very much liked by all Mr. Tennant's scholars.

The parish school, which was situated immediately below the old parish church, was conducted by Mr. Peter M'Laren; but his situation was quite *a sinecure*, as, when the Academy opened, his school was almost deserted. Parish teachers, however, were secure for life in their situations, and he continued in it till his death.

Mr. George Rennie (a native of Alva, and well known along the foot of the Ochils) visited Dollar every year, and conducted singing classes. Mr. Rennie was blind, but had a wonderful gift of knowing people from the sound of their voices. He was a good singer, and was always ready and willing to assist at any concert in the district when his services were asked; and his name was very frequently to be seen on the programme on such occasions.

Mr. Christie (who belonged to Kincardine) was the principal dancing-master in those days, and held his classes in the large public room of the Big Toll-house. He visited Dollar regularly for a long series of years.

From the roll-book of the late Mr. Walker, English teacher, I am enabled (through the kindness of Miss Walker) to give the names of those in my class in the month of April 1831. They are as follows:—

Joseph Martin.	William Gibson.
Paul Forrester.	David Keir.
David Arnot.	George H. Gibson.
James Wardlaw.	Richard Pinkerton.
Peter Blackwood.	William Elliot.
William Ramsay.	Alexander Ledingham.
James Monteath.	George Ledingham.
David Bone.	George Edmonstone.
James Martin.	John Kidd.

The following are the names of some of the boys attending the Academy at the same time as myself, those residing in the district being given first:—

*John Drysdale.
Adam Drysdale.
Robert Drysdale.
William Drysdale.
James Drysdale.
William Elliot.
Alexander Elliot.
John Elliot.
Henry Elliot.
Thomas Porteous.
Charles Erskine.
Robert Young.
Richard Pinkerton.
William Pinkerton.
Thomas Allan.
John Allan.
Dalhousie Allan.
Adam Allan.
William Allan.
David Drysdale.
Thomas Drysdale.
Robert Drysdale.
Robert Shiells.
Thomas Buchanan.
James Henderson.
John Henderson.
Alexander Henderson.
William Lawson.
Daniel Lawson.
Archibald Swan.
John Murray.
Thomas Murray.
George Murray.
David Westwood.
James Robertson.
John Halley.
William Halley.
Peter Blackwood.
Benjamin Taylor.
James Halley.
David Livingston.
George Sharp.
George Halley.
Peter Halley.

Thomas Kirk.
John Kirk.
John Kidd.
Alexander Kidd.
Thomas Kidd.
Adam Kidd.
William Cadogan.
George Cadogan.
Henry Cadogan.
David Arnot.
Henry Arnot.
Robert Arnot.
Alfred Arnot.
*Robert Wright.
John Wright.
William Wright.
James Wright.
George H. Gibson.
John Gibson.
*John Forrester.
*James Forrester.
*Paul Forrester.
William Forrester.
William Walker.
Andrew Walker.
James Walker.
John Syme.
James Christie.
James M'Gruther.
William M'Gruther.
James Wardlaw.
Alexander Wardlaw.
Andrew Campbell.
John Burns.
John M'Nee.
Peter M'Nee.
Robert M'Nee.
David M'Gregor.
Alexander M'Gregor.
James Smeaton.
Robert Carmichael.
Thomas Smeaton.
*Adam Carmichael.
James Carmichael.

John Carmichael.
David Carmichael.
William Cameron.
William Smeaton.
Robert Thomson.
Thomas Thomson.
James Hutcheson.
William Somerville.
John Somerville.
George Anderson.
John Young.
George Tod.
John Sinclair.
Peter Stalker.
Joseph Sharp.
Henry Christie.
John Christie.
James Taylor.
John Taylor.
George Taylor.
Robert Dickie.
William Halley.
James Scotland.
John Scotland.
John Sorely.
John Blackwood.
Alexander Blackwood.
James Blackwood.
William Blackwood.
John M'Iver.
William M'Iver.
Alexander Scott.
John Scott.
Andrew Morgan.
Peter Stewart.
Christopher Seton.
Alexander Ritchie.
Alexander Blackwood.
William Keir.

David Keir.
John Keir.
Robert Keir.
Gordon Keir.
George Haldane.
James Haldane.
David Taylor.
*Campbell Taylor.
George Monteath.
Thomas Monteath.
James Monteath.
John Mercer.
Archibald Mercer.
John Finlayson.
David Finlayson.
John Younger.
Hugh Ross.
James Hardie.
Alexander Drysdale.
Thomas Drysdale.
James Jack.
John Jack.
Henry Wardlaw.
Robert Wright.
James Syme.
Robert Syme.
John Syme.
Henry Syme.
James Gibson.
Henry Gibson.
John Stewart.
Peter Stewart.
James Syme.
William Syme.
Gilbert Martin.
William Martin.
James Martin.
James Crombie.
Frederick Crombie.

For a great many years a silver-handled penknife was presented annually by a gentleman as a prize for the best writer in the Academy; and I have put an asterisk at the names of the accomplished eight who gained this distinguished honour, viz. John Drysdale, Harviestoun; Robert Wright, Gateside, Dollar; John, James, and Paul Forrester, Dollar; Adam Carmichael, Dollar; and Campbell Taylor, Castle Campbell. I have only been able to ascertain the name of one boarder who gained this distinguished honour, viz. James Ronald from Kirkcaldy (now of Newport), but doubtless some of the others would gain it also. One of the Messrs. Hogg, of Valleyfield, has been mentioned—by an old schoolfellow—as one of the successful competitors, but as he had left the Academy before my day, I cannot vouch for the correctness of this.

BOARDERS.

Robert Ward.
Joseph Ward.
John Mackie.
Andrew M'Queen.
John M. M'Queen.
Archibald M'Queen.
Daniel M'Queen.
John W. Watson.
Henry Calman.
David Cowan.
Archibald Hogg.
David Bone.
Alexander Somerville.
Andrew Mallach.
Donald M'Glashan.
George Russell.
*James Ronald.
David Ferguson.
John M. Reeve.
George Brown.
Robert Inglis.
James Campbell.
John Ramsay.
Robert Ramsay.

David Ramsay.
William Campbell.
Robert Millie.
Robert Pinkerton.
James Stewart.
James Alston.
David Alston.
Edward Mitchell.
John Stewart.
Alexander Thomson.
Douglas M'Murdoch.
John Ingram.
Thomas Adamson.
Thomas Young.
Robert Young.
Robert Paterson.
Andrew Paterson.
Adam Kirk.
Joseph Bourne.
George Edmonstone.
Charles Horsburgh.
Boyd Horsburgh.
John Horsburgh.
Richard Bell.

Thomas Bell.	Jasper Robertson.
Alexander Rankine.	Robert Drysdale.
Henry Rankine.	John Drysdale.
Andrew Campbell.	Alexander Ledingham.
James Wylie.	George Ledingham.
Walter Wylie.	Robert Walker.
Thomas Naughton Cox.	Joseph Martin.
Charles Robertson.	William Martin.
William Robertson.	Thomas Martin.
Thomas Spiers.	Edward Wolff.
James Spiers.	George Wolff.
Alexander Robertson.	

Could the biographies of all on these two lists of names be written, they would, I have no doubt, form a series of very interesting volumes, exemplifying in many instances the truth of the old adage, 'that truth is often stranger than fiction.'

As a specimen of the arbitrary conduct of the Rev. Dr. Mylne, Robert and William M'Leish (now of Tillicoultry), sons of John M'Leish (who took an active part, along with a great many of the inhabitants, in opposing the Doctor in some of his schemes), were refused admission into the Academy, and had, for a time, to walk all the way to Muckart to attend school; and when they attended a night-school in Dollar, under the auspices of the Trustees of the Academy, they were charged fees, while the other parish boys got this education free.

THE REV. DR. WYLLIE.

Dollar had in those days for one of its ministers a gentleman whose fame as an author has now become ' world-wide,' the Rev. Dr. Wyllie. His church (generally called 'The Auld Licht'), situated to the east of Cairnpark Street, has now been turned into two dwellinghouses, and is known by the name of Mayfield. He married Miss Gray, sister of Mr. Gray, the mathematical teacher.

I recollect well of an amusing incident in connection with the Doctor's church, which showed how tenaciously old folks cling to antiquated customs, and how any innovation is looked on with so much suspicion. In early times, when education was not so general as it is now, and very many were unable to read, it was the custom for precentors to read every line of the psalm before singing it; and this had evidently got to be considered as essential in singing the praises of the sanctuary. Well, at an evening service one night, a stranger precentor was leading the praise, and he couldn't, it seemed, do this, but sang straight on without reading, or, as it was called in those days, singing 'run-line;' when, after he had got one verse finished in this heretical style, a great commotion was observed at the head of one of the seats right in front of the pulpit, and a good old lady of the old town was seen crushing out past the rest of the folks in the seat, and hurried down the long passage as fast as her legs could carry her, and, after getting the door opened, dashed it to behind her with all her might, to show her indignation at such open profanity in her 'ain gude Auld Licht Kirk.' What a fine neighbour she would have made to a certain Free Church divine of the present day! It is really wonderful how *he* ever allowed 'run-line' to be sung.

It would have been very amusing to have seen the effect of an organ on this old lady in Dollar Church, could it have been got to start, unexpectedly, to accompany the precentor in the praise. If 'run-line' was bad, the organ would have been something dreadful, and nothing less than a fit of hysterics could have been looked for. But, indeed, we need scarcely be surprised that this would have been the result fifty years ago, when we think that the consequences would almost certainly be the same to a good many 'reverend auld wives' and their followers of the present day; for no matter although David used all sorts of instruments in the service of the sanctuary, and that there are instruments in heaven (Rev. xiv. 2), your 'Use-and-Wont' man says no such thing as an organ must be thought of, for it is both 'unscriptural' and 'sinful' to do so. I am convinced, however, that this old prejudice against the aid of an organ or harmonium in singing God's praise, will in course of time die out, in the same way as that which at one time existed against singing 'run-line.' Just think of one of our great doctors of divinity of the present day prohibiting his hearers, wherever he preaches, from standing when singing God's praise, because the old antiquated custom was to sit! So much for prejudice and bigotry.

In his *Annals and Statistics of the U.P. Church*, Dr. M'Kelvie tells us that so determined was the opposition to the introduction of singing 'run-line,' that congregations were split up by it, and that the persons seceding on this account from the churches in the parishes of Tough and Johnshaven were so numerous as to form congregations at once.

If our 'Purity of Worship Association' of the present day had existed in those days, we would have found it fighting against the innovation of 'run-line' with all the pertinacious bigotry of some of its leaders, and making themselves, as at present, the 'laughing-stock' of the greater portion of the community.

ORIGIN OF THE NAME OF CAIRNPARK IN DOLLAR.

I have just learned, in the course of my present inquiries, that at the beginning of this century Dollar was possessed of an object of very great interest, but which unfortunately was entirely removed about the year 1806 or 1807. This was nothing less than a great pyramid (well, it was not quite so big as the famous one of Egypt, but still it was a great pile) which had evidently been erected to commemorate some great battle, or the death of some celebrated warrior; and it certainly is very much to be regretted that it should have been removed. This was an immense cairn of stones, some thirty feet high, and as many square at the base; and the park in which it stood took its name from it—Cairnpark; and the street leading up to the Academy also got its name—Cairnpark Street—from its being made through this park. It will scarcely be believed, yet it is nevertheless true, that this ancient and interesting cairn was removed for the ignoble purpose of being broken into road-metal for the new turnpike road that was then being constructed along the foot of the Ochils. By whose orders it was removed I cannot say; but the late Mr. William Blackwood, of the New Town, superintended its removal, and kept a correct note of the cart-loads that were in it, and found they amounted to the astonishing number of one thousand!

When the bottom was reached, there were found in the centre of it a number of ancient clay urns, showing that this immense cairn was a thing of great antiquity, and connected with some important event, and, had it been allowed to remain, would have been an object of interest second only to Castle Campbell itself, and an additional attraction to the ancient town of Dollar. The Rev. Mr. Watson got possession of some of the urns, but what became of them is not now known.

The street in which Mayfield now stands had then only the one one-storied house (Mrs. M'Lean's) and Park House (where the late Mrs. Kirk and family then lived) to the east of the church, and the entrance to it from the east was at the end of Park House, from the back road. It was not till Dr. Arnot built the house to the east of Park House, that the street was opened up to the burn-side. With the exception of Dr. Wyllie's church, the one-storied house referred to, and Park House, there were no houses to the east of Cairnpark Street but those on Bridge Street—all being green fields.

The corner park, where Mr. Gibb's house and garden now stand, used to be unenclosed, and a near cut was generally taken across it, from Bridge Street to the burn-side. It was in this open field we used to have glorious ' bonfires ' on the King's birthday.

OLD FAMILIES OF DOLLAR, ETC.

I will now refer shortly to one of the most influential and highly-respected families of Dollar—the Haigs of Dollarfield. With the exception of the wool mill, Dollar bleachfield was the only other public work in Dollar, and a great number of the inhabitants got employment at it. I have a very distinct recollection of the worthy founder of those prosperous works (which were commenced in 1787), William Haig, Esq. (the present Mr. Haig's grandfather), who was a man of sterling worth, and highly respected by the whole community of Dollar. He was a justice of the peace for the county of Clackmannan. Mrs. Haig, also, who was a most amiable, kind, motherly lady, I remember very well. Mr. Haig died in 1834, and Mrs. Haig in 1849.

Mr. James Haig, their eldest son, died in 1832, and left a widow to lament his early death, who was very much respected in Dollar, but who has, for long been non-resident in it.

I cannot bring Mr. James Haig's appearance to my recollection, but Mr. Robert Haig (the present Mr. Haig's father) I remember very well. He was a most excellent man, and had at heart all that concerned the best interests of the inhabitants of Dollar. Besides being a Trustee of Dollar Academy, he was a justice of the peace, and Deputy-Lieutenant of the county of Clackmannan. He died in 1854. Mrs. Robert Haig (a lady much esteemed by all) predeceased her husband by seventeen years; she died in 1837.

Of Miss Haig, who died in 1869, and Miss Mary Ann Haig, who died in 1873 (aunts of the present Mr. Haig), it would be impossible for me to speak too highly, for two more excellent ladies could not be found anywhere. Their many acts of kindness will be long remembered in Dollar.

Mr. Haig is proprietor of the fine estates of Glensherup and Dollarfield.

I will only mention one place of amusement connected with my school days, that will be fondly remembered by every one who has attended Dollar Academy, and which is still cherished as a favourite place of resort by the present generation, and that is 'The Dead Waters'—a large field immediately below Devon Grove (the late Professor Tennant's house), that was flooded every winter, and where skating, curling, and every sort of ice amusements were carried on. The quickest road to it, and the one we generally took, was through 'The Scott's Plantain,' along by the side of the 'Quarrel Burn,' the stream which is used for flooding this field.

In the Old Town, the next two-storied house to my father's on the north was occupied for a very long time by the Misses Young (three sisters), who were very much respected in Dollar; and their brother, Mr. George Young, and family, were prominent members of our community, and highly esteemed by every one. Miss Isabella Young, Mr. George's daughter, is the only one who now represents this worthy family in Dollar. The Misses Young's garden adjoined my father's to the north.

At the head of the old town lived Mr. John Mathie (generally called 'Provost Mathie'), a very worthy, good old man, who lived to the long age of ninety-six years. Although in my young days Dollar was not ruled by a provost and magistrates, it had been at one time, and for a very long period, under a provost and baron bailies; and, counting from his time, Mr. Mathie's ancestors had been provost, in succession, for three hundred years. Although at that time, therefore, he was not invested with the powers of a chief magistrate, the old title was still kept up, and even descended to one of his sons. As long as he was able, he used to pay daily visits to my father's shop, and I remember him very well.

Amongst the last of those who acted as baron bailies in the end of last century, when Castle Campbell was still in the possession of the Duke of Argyle, three of them lived till just before my day, and one of them ('Old Hillie') I used to hear often spoken of. Their names are as follows :—

John Marshall, farmer.
James Sharp, smith.
John Drysdale, flesher.

John Drysdale was at one time proprietor of Hillfoot, and hence got the name of ' Old Hillie.' He resided latterly in the open square, to the north of my father's house in Dollar, and it was known in those days as ' Hillie's Close.' ' Deacon Gibson' (William—a well-known man in Dollar) lived also in this square. James Lawson (a son of Emily Gibson's) lived in the house at the east side of the square, on the rising ground, and at the junction of the two streets.

An amusing story used to be told about one of the Provost's daughters—Jenny. A Willie Rutherford and she courted each other for thirty years; and when at last they got married, Jenny used to say 'that her marriage came on her a' in a dunt.' What Jenny would have considered a leisurely courtship, it is really hard to say, but most folks would have considered the time she took ample.

Opposite my father's house were the Cross Keys Inn and the house of John Blackwood, the celebrated fiddler, This John Blackwood had three brothers, who were, along with himself, famous throughout the country as violin players, and were taken far and near to balls and dances of all kinds. John, James, and Robert played the violin, and Tom the violoncello; and for Scotch reels and strathspeys, this band could not be excelled by any one in the country. The ' Blackwoods of Dollar' were as well known and celebrated in those days as ' Adams' band' is at the present time. Their musical talent has, I learn, descended to the second and third generations. Thomas and Robert (' Ebony '), sons of John (both resident in Canada), have inherited their father's gift, and are both good violin players. John also (resident in Dollar)—a son of Thomas (one of the famous band)—plays, I understand, very well; and Thomas (resident in Hawick)—a grandson of John's—is an excellent player.

While referring to the Blackwoods, it may not be out of place here to relate a story I have heard about a celebrated fiddler who lived in Dollar long before my time, and from whom, very likely, the Blackwoods may have got their first lessons in fiddling. In the end of last century, the Duke of Argyle invited a number of famous fiddlers to a competition in his town mansion in Edinburgh (Argyle House), when a goodly number made their appearance, and amongst the rest, one Johnnie Cook, from Dollar.

To prevent any partiality, the fiddlers were arranged behind a screen, and each in his turn played some tunes before a large audience. After all had performed, the first prize was unanimously awarded to Johnnie Cook, and resulted in a large sum of money being subscribed for him on the spot; and he came back to Dollar with a goodly sum in his pocket. The question then with Johnnie was, in what way could he best invest his newly-acquired wealth? and thinking, no doubt, that land was safer than any other investment (banks and other companies often coming to grief), he bought a field to the east of the old town of Dollar with it, which was at once dubbed by the good folks of Dollar, Fiddlefield; and by this name it continues to be known to the present day.

That this Johnnie Cook must have been considered no unimportant personage in Dollar, may be gathered from a story told of John Orr, a well-known old pensioner in Dollar in my young days. When John landed,

H

with his regiment, in Egypt, about the year 1800, he found one David Lambert, another Dollar man, there before him; and being anxious, no doubt, to communicate the most startling bit of news he had brought with him, he at once asked Lambert 'if he had heard the news.' When told he had heard nothing, the great and important event was then made known to him—not that Napoleon Bonaparte was killed, but that 'Johnnie Cook, the fiddler, was dead.' We can picture to ourselves the two worthies mingling their tears together over the termination of the life of so celebrated a man, and thinking, no doubt, that the glory of Dollar had departed.

John Orr and Lambert were under the command of Sir Ralph Abercrombie, and would, no doubt, take part in the great battle of Alexandria, fought on March 21, 1801, when the British gained such a signal victory over the French, and let Napoleon see what sort of stuff British troops were made of.

When John Orr came home from the war, he astonished the good folks of Dollar with his wonderful stories about Egypt—about there being three crops in the year, etc.; and I remember well how the boys used to run after the old pensioner, and tease him, by shouting his name two or three times, and then adding, 'Three crops in Egypt;' which invariably roused his ire to the highest pitch, and would have led to broken bones had they not got out of his way.

When John was asked any question that he was not quite sure about, he was never much at a loss for an answer. On being asked, one day, if he ever saw the Pyramids when in Egypt, he at once replied, 'Oh yes; we took them prisoners.'

John, it seems, had been a sore grief to Mr. M'Arbrea

when at his school, and used to play truant and all
sorts of tricks; and on one occasion, when things had
reached a crisis, his mother had to be sent for. To the
dominie's surprise, Mrs. Orr brought a rope in her hand,
and seeing little hope, I suppose, of reformation, she
handed it to Mr. M'Arbrea, and told him to hang him
with it, and if he wouldn't do it, another would. It
seems, however, that when it 'came to the scratch' John
had got round his mother's heart in some way, for the
dreadful threat was not carried into execution, and he
was spared to serve his King and his country.

THE HORSE-SHOE, AND WESTERN SUBURBS OF DOLLAR, ETC.

On entering Dollar from the west, the first house
approached was a rather peculiar one—a substantial
one-storied house, with a very wide door, in the shape
of a horse-shoe, which was built by Mr. Tait, of Harviestoun, for a smithy, and carried on as such for many
a year. It was a well-known landmark, on account of
its peculiarly-shaped door, and was always spoken of
(and still is by the old inhabitants of Dollar) as 'The
Horse-Shoe.' Harviestoun Villa now occupies its site.

The next house on the high road—Belmont—was for
a long period occupied by Dr. Elliot's widow and family,
and Miss Elliot was one of the sprightliest and most
spirited young ladies of our Dollar society. There were
four sons and five daughters—William, Alexander, John,
Henry, Margaret, Helen, Jane, Jemima, and Louisa.
The Doctor died in 1834.

Captain Porteous' house, Mount Devon, comes next.
I cannot recall the Captain to memory; but Mrs. and
Miss Porteous and Tom will always be associated in

my memory with this house. Miss Porteous was a
very superior young lady, and lived for a long time in
the house alone, after her mother's death. She married
a Mr. Beveridge. Thomas commenced business in
Glasgow, but died when quite a young man, leaving a
widow and young family to mourn his early death. He
was a very pushing young man, and, had he been spared,
would have soon taken a prominent position amongst
the successful merchants of Glasgow.

The present occupants of the cottage below Mount
Devon (Belville)—Mr. William and Miss Drysdale—
are associated with my earliest recollections of Harviestoun Castle, and the home farm adjoining it, where the
family so long resided. I do not recollect much of Mr.
Drysdale, their father (who was so long factor for Mr.
Tait); but Mrs. Drysdale, who survived her husband for
twenty-three years, was a most kind, amiable lady, and
much esteemed by every one who knew her. On the
death of his father in 1843, Mr. William succeeded to
the factorship, and acted in that capacity till the estate
passed out of the hands of the Globe Insurance Company. Two brothers, Robert and Adam, went to the
West Indies, and died there—Robert in 1835, and
Adam in 1839. Mr. John died in Belville Cottage in
1860. Mr. James Drysdale, banker, Stirling, is the
youngest brother.

An amusing story is told of a goat and gander that
were long amongst Mrs. Drysdale's collection of live
stock at Harviestoun. A strong and lasting attachment
sprang up between the two; and wherever Nannie was
to be seen, there was the gander, his natural companions,
the geese, being, in a most *ungentlemanly* way, invariably 'left out in the cold.'

When Mrs. Drysdale and family left Harviestoun,

and took up their residence in Belville Cottage, the goat and gander were made a present of to Mr. Henderson, of the Castle Campbell Hotel in Dollar; and the same strong attachment continued between the two as before, the goat never being seen anywhere without his companion. Well, one Sabbath day this worthy couple took it into their heads that they would like to hear what kind of a preacher the Rev. Mr. Craigie was; and just as the congregation in the Established Church had nearly all assembled, and the advent of the minister into the pulpit was momentarily looked for, who should march slowly along one of the passages, but Nannie and his companion the gander, and, in order to make sure of hearing well, went right up the pulpit stair, and apparently were bent on getting into the pulpit itself.

As may be readily imagined, the arrival of such unexpected and distinguished visitors created the greatest excitement and amusement in the church——to all except the poor beadle, who seemed to view the situation of affairs in absolute dismay. What was to be done? The gander was known to be of a very pugnacious disposition, and resented at once the slightest interference with his companion; and for any stranger to have attempted to forcibly eject Nannie would have been sheer madness. The church officer was fairly at his wits' end what to do, when fortunately Mr. William Drysdale (who happened to be in church) came to the rescue. Rising out of his seat, he approached the worthy couple, and calling the goat by name, told it to follow him. Remembering its old master thoroughly well, it at once obeyed his order, and the two were quietly walked out of the church, to the no little amusement and great relief of all concerned. How to explain the very singular and strong attachment that existed between these two, I must leave to some of my ornithological friends, who are more skilled in these matters than I am.

What subsequently became of them is not recorded in history; but we must be left to suppose that, after reaching a good old age, they both died a natural death, faithfully attached to each other to the last.

Mrs. Hynd, Dollar, informs me that she was present in the Established Church when this most ludicrous scene took place, and it really was a most amusing spectacle.

Broomrig, the next house in order, was in my young days occupied by a Mrs. Young and family; and Robert, one of her sons, was a class-fellow of mine. Miss Young got married at a very early age to an Edinburgh gentleman. It was after they left that it was then occupied by the Honourable David Erskine and family. There was only the centre house at that time—the extensive additions to and adjoining it having since been made by the present proprietor—James Leishman, Esq.

Devonside House (so long occupied by Mrs. M'Callum and family) comes next, which was built by a Captain Pinkerton, a stout, military-looking man, with pure white hair. Miss Pinkerton—a nice young girl of fifteen—was cut off after a few hours' illness, in the year 1833. Mrs. Pinkerton died in 1835.

Devongrove—close to the Dead Waters—and Springfield have been referred to already. Mr. and Mrs. Martin had no family; and I recollect well of them sitting in the front square seat of the west gallery of the old church (along with the Honourable David Erskine and family), right above where they now lie buried.

Woodcot was built by the late Dr. Walker, uncle of the present doctor, who was for a very long period the principal medical man of the district, and was considered a man of great skill, and very much esteemed. He died in the year 1844.

The centre house of Helen Place was for a considerable time occupied by Mr. Bell (son-in-law of the late Mrs. Duncanson of Sheardale, as an educational establishment (styled by him Broomfield Academy), and a very large number attended his classes there. He commenced this establishment after resigning his situation in Dollar Academy of mathematical teacher. He had a large number of boarders, and two of them are very distinctly impressed on my memory as spirited young boys — Charles Davis and Henry Ogilvie. In what part of the world, I wonder, will those two be now ? or are they—like so many, so very many, of my school companions—in their graves ?

Between Helen Place and the old toll-bar there were, for many a long day, only the one one-storied house at the east end of Charlotte Place (Mr. William M'Leish's), and the cottage to the west of the other end of it. This cottage was built by a Mr. Mallach, manager in Dollar Bleachfield, and it was always spoken of as ' Mallach's Cottage.' By and by the fine two-storied house to the west of it (Viewfield) was built by a Mrs. Allan, for herself and large family, after leaving the farm of Dollar Bank, which they had occupied for a considerable time. This large and highly-respected family occupied for long a very prominent place in our Dollar society, and many happy evenings I have spent in their house. Mrs. Allan was a most hospitable, kind lady, and very much esteemed by every one ; and some of the happiest days of my youth are associated with her and her worthy family. Their names were as follows : Thomas, John, Dalhousie, Adam, William, Elizabeth, Janet, Helen (Mrs. Beveridge), Ann (Mrs. Grieve), Alison (Mrs Bathgate), Christina (Mrs. Drysdale), Mary (Mrs. Wilson), Eliza, and Jane Darling—fourteen in all. Three only of this large family now remain, viz. Mrs. Bathgate, Miss Eliza, and Miss Jeanie, the last only being now resident in Dollar. Mrs. Allan died at Liverpool (where Mrs. Wilson resided) in 1847.

The first occupant of Castle Campbell Hotel that I remember of was Mr. Alexander Henderson, grandfather of Mr. Henderson, writer, Alloa. Mrs. Henderson was a sister of Provost Foreman's of Stirling, and a very worthy lady. After Mr. Henderson's death, it was for a considerable period carried on by his son-in-law, Mr. John Robertson; and, after his death, by Mr. John Henderson, son of old Mr. Henderson.

GLOOMHILL AND HILLFOOT, ETC.

Very many of my Saturday afternoons (we had to go to school on Saturday forenoon in those ·days) were spent up at Gloomhill farmhouse with Alick and Johnnie Scott, my school companions, where we used to have some rare fun with old Mr. Robert Cram's donkey, which, though the most docile and serviceable of creatures to its venerable master, knew thoroughly well how to tumble off troublesome boys; and many a good ' header ' we got from it.

Mr. John Scott's family consisted of four—Grace, Alexander, John, and Marion. Grace married a Mr. Currer of Ardross, an extensive and successful farmer in the neighbourhood of Elie, Fife. Alexander is settled in Stratford, Ontario, Upper Canada, and his family are grown up and getting on well in the world. John was drowned in Australia, on December 23, 1853; and Miss Scott alone is now left in Dollar. Mr. Scott was overseer on Hillfoot estate.

Mr. Peter Cram, merchant, New Town, and Mr. David Cram, Alloa, are sons of old Mr. Cram, who was tenant of the hill farm of Hillfoot—John M'Arthur Moir, Esq., being at that time the proprietor of the estate of Hillfoot. No finer view of Dollar and Castle Campbell can be got anywhere than from the top of Gloomhill.

When I was at school, Mr. Moir was a widower, and his sister Miss Moir kept house for him. Four nephews of the name of M'Queen lived with him for a number of years, and attended Dollar Academy, viz. Andrew, John, Archibald, and Daniel. They were bright, lively, nice-dispositioned boys.

There being no poor law in existence in those days, the only public way of raising money for the maintenance of the poor was the collections at the Established Church doors. The plate at the old church of Dollar stood a few yards *out* from the session-house door, so as to be convenient for the folks in passing; while the elder stood *in* the door. These collections not being required for the support of the minister, a good many people passed the plate without giving anything; and when it was Mr. Moir's turn to stand, and he saw people passing without giving, whom he knew were very well able to give, and who generally bowed to him in passing, he was not slack in reminding them of their duty, and used to bawl out to them, 'Mind the plate, mind the plate, never mind me!' to the great amusement of the bystanders and the no little confusion of the party addressed. One worthy man, still living in Dollar, I heard one day thus addressed by name, and he went away into the church looking anything but comfortable.

Mr. Moir was an artist of considerable skill, and I recollect well of him taking a sketch one day, in the Academy grounds, of The Banks and Dollar Hill, and in the course of his picture was putting in a paling at a very quick rate; when, turning round to a number of us boys who were looking on, he asked, 'Do you think you could drive in paling stobs as fast as that?' which of course put us all into good humour, and caused great merriment, which was just what Mr. Moir wanted, as he always enjoyed a good laugh. He was a good-hearted, kind landlord, and, in addition to his estate of Hillfoot, was proprietor of the fine estate of Milton, at Dunoon. He was a justice of the peace for the county of Clackmannan, and being one of the elders in the Established Church, was, as already stated, a trustee of Dollar Academy. He died at Hillfoot on December 17, 1871, aged seventy-three years.

The session-house of the old church still stands to the south of the entrance gate.

Mr. Alexander Stalker (father of Mr. Peter Stalker, who was so long and so well known in Dollar) carried on the wright trade in the old town. He lived in the two-storied house almost opposite the present Lorne Tavern; and his workshop was in the one-storied house adjoining, now turned into a dwelling-house. His family consisted of five—Isabella, Peter, Jane, Margaret, and Agnes (Mrs. Hynd).

The first house on the left-hand side, on entering the cart-road to the Castle, was a well-known house in Dollar, and amongst the farmers around—the smithy and dwelling-house of Andrew Sharp, senior. His son Andrew was in business with his father, but was married, and lived in the house next the Castle wood, and close to the Broomie Knowe. This smithy was a great resort of the youths of the village, and many an hour I have sat by the smithy fire and looked on at the red-hot bars being hammered away. Old Andrew, who was very fond of a joke, quite alarmed my good old grandmother one day by telling her, when getting a refreshment, and when about to turn over his glass, that her whisky 'was on the turn.'

Any notice of the old town of Dollar as it existed fifty years ago would be incomplete without referring to a very harmless 'character' we had amongst us, who was well known, and made welcome to every house in Dollar—Robbie Guild. Nothing delighted Robbie more than to get a book (particularly the Bible) to read, and a most amusing job he made of it. One of his peculiarities was that, when reading, he could not get past certain words, and would repeat and re-repeat the half of a sentence a dozen of times over before he could make out to finish it, which was very amusing; and of course Robbie was often asked to read. The same sort of difficulty occurred to him when walking about. He would stop suddenly for a considerable time, then lift the offending stone or bit of straw, and carry it to the side of the road, and when the obstacle was removed would then proceed on his way. When teased by boys, he occasionally got into a great fury, and was then (as any one would have been) rather dangerous; but when let alone, he was of a mild and harmless disposition, and was kindly treated by every one in Dollar.

Another well-known 'character' in those days was

Willie Stewart, who was sadly teased by the boys, and his life made very miserable by some of them. Willie used to go messages, and do many little jobs for a number of families, and was very frequently on the road, and was thus much exposed to his tormentors. He had a strong burr, and I think the boys liked to hear Willie ' burring ' out his remonstrances. He was a simple, good-hearted body, and it was a great shame to see the way he was often abused.

He hadn't—as an auld Scotch saying goes—' enough o' the deil in him, to keep the deil aff him,' for had he given some of them a good sound thrashing some day, he would soon have put a stop to it. But Willie would rather run when he could, than fight, and tried always to get out of their way. When the scholars were going home from the Academy one night, Willie was heard saying to himself, ' Therre thae rroyd laddies comin' again ; I'll awa' up to the high rroad, and no' be tormented be them.'

Mr. Wilson, baker, carried on a prosperous business in the Old Town, from which he retired a good many years ago. He married the eldest daughter of Mr. John Swan, merchant, New Town.

The other members of Mr. Swan's family were Mary, Jessie, Helen (first Mrs. Robert Shiells, Neenah, America), and Archibald, who were all among my school companions. Mrs. Wilson, Mary, and Jessie are still in Dollar, but Archibald has been long settled in America.

Mr. Robert Kirk (one of the Trustees of the Academy) was a very worthy man, and much respected in Dollar. He carried on the wright trade, and at the same time had a shop in the south street of the Old Town. Besides a son who died when young, he had other four of a family—Margaret, John, Thomas, and Catherine. Miss Kirk alone now survives.

I might fill a volume were I to go in detail over all the old families of Dollar, but will finish my list by simply mentioning one or two others.

Dr. Martin's family—Gilbert, William, James, Anne, etc. The Doctor died in Malta in 1843.

Dr. Arnot's family—David, Henry, Robert, Alfred, and Margaret (Mrs. Wilson). The Doctor died in 1842, aged fifty-seven.

Late Mrs. Kirk's family, Park House—Elizabeth (Mrs. James Kirk, Tullibody), Catherine (Mrs. Robert Wright, Greenock), Thomas, and John.

Mrs. Kid's family—Helen, Jane (Mrs. M'Nair), John, Alexander, Thomas, and Adam. They lived in the first house to the east of the New Club House, which is now joined to the large block of new buildings, but stood at that time by itself.

Mrs. Burns' family, of the Old Town—Eliza (first Mrs. Peter Stalker), Ann, and John. Mrs. Burns died in 1850, and John in 1848. Her husband died in 1827.

The principal grocers in the New Town fifty years ago were Mr. Hugh Munro and Mr. John Swan. Mr. Charles Lawson was the only draper.

There was no regular post office in Dollar at that time, but Mr. Robert Forrester (who then lived in Cairnpark Street) received the letters into his house, and carried them to the post office in Alloa, and brought back the letters from there on his return. The first post-master appointed to Dollar was Mr. John Philip, in 1830; and when he died in 1838, his daughter, Miss Philip, succeeded him, and continued post-mistress till her death. Their post office was in the house close to the old toll-bar.

CHAPTER VI.

RELATIVES AT ONE TIME IN CLACKMANNAN.

I WILL now refer more particularly than I have yet
done to my worthy Aunt Sarah of Clackmannan, my
mother's eldest sister, and Uncle Henry. She had a
passionate love for the place of her birth—Bankhead,
of Tullibole ; and many were the stories she used to
tell us of the folks round about there—in Hood's Hill,
Coldrain, the Gelvin, etc. ; and so vivid were the pictures of some of the scenes she described, that you got
to have quite an interest in the whole locality.

She was an exceedingly cheerful person, and her
merry laugh could be heard a great way off ; and so
much was she esteemed, generally, in the town of her
adoption, that there wasn't one in it, I believe, but
would have done her a kind turn if they had had it in
their power.

She attended the ministry of the Rev. Mr. Balfour
(the present Lord Advocate's father), and from both
him and Mrs. Balfour she ever received the greatest
kindness. She used frequently to speak of the faithful
visits paid her, along with others, of Mrs. Bruce of
Kennet (Lord Burleigh's mother), and the many excellent tracts she left with them. She died, as I have
already mentioned, in 1862, aged seventy-nine.

Uncle Henry lived with her till his death in 1833.
Besides being of a decidedly poetical turn of mind, he

was very fond of painting, and, though self-taught, produced some most creditable pictures, some of which adorned their rooms. One, particularly, of Alva House and the Wood Hill, in oil, was a very well-executed painting indeed, and a most faithful representation of the scene.

The farm of Bankhead was sold by my Grandfather Wilson to Lord Moncreiff about the year 1820. My brother in Dollar being anxious to become possessed of the property which once belonged to his forefathers, bought it back from Lord Moncreiff in 1859, and held possession of it for twenty-one years. In 1880 he sold it to the late Robert Mowbray, Esq., of Naemoor, to whose family it now belongs.

SOJOURN IN DUNFERMLINE.

In the year 1835 I left school, and commenced the business of life. I went to Dunfermline, and served a three years' apprenticeship to the drapery trade, with Mr. David Inglis, Bridge Street ; and was afterwards about a year in Stewart & M'Donald's, in Glasgow.

During my sojourn in Dunfermline, I had the pleasure (along with my companions who lived in the same apartments with me) of getting introduced to some very nice, kind families ; amongst others, I may mention Mr. Joseph Paton, Wooer's Alley ; Mr. Bonar, builder ; Mr. Hay, St. Margaret Street ; Mrs. Auld, High Street, etc.

Mr. Joseph Paton (Sir Noel Paton's father) was a great antiquarian, and his house was filled with a most valuable collection of old armour, antique furniture, etc., and visitors came from far and near to see his collection, and were always made welcome. Mrs. Paton was one of the kindest and most motherly of ladies, and many a happy evening we spent in their house.

Mr. Paton, I recollect, was very anxious that Robert Wright and I (both Dollar lads) should make a thorough search about the nooks and corners of Castle Campbell, and see if no old relic could be discovered; and I remember well of taking down to him a bit of an old saddle I found in one of the dungeons of the keep, and of which I was sure I had made 'a great find;' but, to my great mortification, it turned out to be a bit of a very modern saddle indeed, and all my high expectations regarding it were suddenly blighted.

The fine ruins of the old Palace and old Abbey Church of the ancient city of Dunfermline (connected as it is with the earliest of the kings and queens of our Scottish history, as also those of more recent date) are very well worth seeing; and to any one who has not been there, I would say, ' Go and see them.'

During my sojourn there, forty-five years ago, its celebrity as the seat of the manufacture of linen and woollen damask tablecloths, covers, etc., was world-wide, and it was then a very thriving town indeed, and some very extensive businesses were being carried on in it. Since then it has made great strides, and some very large manufactories have been built, and great fortunes realized, by some of its citizens who were then boys.

Mr. William M'Laren (of W. & J. M'Laren) was one of the older hands in Mr. Inglis's shop during my apprenticeship; and Mr. John M'Laren had just left for a situation in Edinburgh, previous to my entering. Mr. William Shaw of Milnathort (now of Neilson, Shaw, & M'Gregor, Glasgow), and Messrs. Robert and

William Wright of Dollar, and I lived together in the
same apartments during our apprenticeships; and Mr.
William Mathieson, Mr. Thomas Bonar, Mr. Noel Paton
(now Sir Noel), Mr. John Cooper, Mr. James Meldrum,
and Messrs. Robert and John Hay, were amongst our
most intimate acquaintances. Mr. Shaw was an ap-
prentice with Colville & Robertson, drapers; and
Messrs. Robert and William Wright were apprentices
with Mr. Thomas Stevenson, writer.

Peter Taylor, Colville & Robertson, Thomas Beveridge,
David Reid (afterwards Reid & Davie), J. & A. Duncanson, David Inglis, David Anderson, and William
Finlayson, were the principal drapers of those days—all
of whom have now passed away. To give an idea how
extensively manufacturing was carried on in Dunfermline at the time of which I write, I will here give
a list of the firms then in existence, which I am
enabled to do through the kindness of an old and
esteemed friend in Dunfermline. John Kinell, Golfdrum; Robert Balfour, Golfdrum; William Hutton, Golfdrum; David Dewar & Co., Woodhead Street; Philip
& Law, Woodhead Street; John Cowper, Pittencrieff
Street; Hay & Shoolbred, Pittencrieff Street; David
Inglis, Bridge Street; James & Alexander Beugo, High
Street; William Hunt & Son, High Street; George
Inglis & Son, East Port Street; James Inglis, East
Port Street; James Blackwood, East Port Street;
William & John Swan, Queen Anne Street; John Dar-
ling, Knabbie Street; James Kirkland, Knabbie Street;
James & Thomas Spence & Co., St. Catherine's Wynd;
David Williamson, Moodie Street; Adam & William
Bowie, Moodie Street; James Hall & Co., Moodie
Street; Thomas Wilson & Sons, Newrow; James Alex-
ander, Canmore Street; Robert & George Birrel, St.

I

Margaret Street; Alexander Bogie, St. Margaret Street; George Burt & Sons, Back of Dam; David Hogg, New-row; Robert & James Kerr, Bruce Street; William Kinnes, Canmore Street; Andrew Peebles, Guildhall Street; Thomas & John Russell, Maygate; Erskine Beveridge, St. Leonard's Works. As showing the great changes that take place in half a century, the friend who has supplied me with this list (most of whom I remember well) informs me that every one on it has now passed away.

The greater part of the fabrics were at that time wrought on the hand-loom, by weavers throughout the town. This is all changed now, and the weaving is nearly all done in large factories on the power-loom, giving employment to some four or five thousand women.

Messrs. Rutherford's thread mills were at that time being carried on with great spirit, their thread having quite a name throughout the country.

Mr. Taylor, Kirkgate, Mr. Gibb, Maygate, Mr. Husband, Queen Anne Street, Mr. Henry Russell, High Street, Mr. William Drummond, High Street, Messrs. J. & A. Beugo, High Street, Mr. Samson, Bridge Street, and Mr. David Blelloch, Maygate, were the principal grocers, the last two only of whom are now left.

The Rev. Mr. Young was minister of Queen Anne Street U.P. Church; Rev. John Law, Rev. G. B. Brand, Rev. William Dalziell, Rev. Mr. Cuthbertson, and Rev. Mr. M'Michael, of other five Dissenting churches; and the Rev. Peter Chalmers, under whom I sat, was minister of the Abbey Church. All the seven have now passed away.

The principal writers were, Mr. Thomas Stevenson, Mr. M'Donald, fiscal, Mr. Strachan, Mr. William Beveridge, sen., Mr. James Smith Ronaldson, Mr. William

Warren, and Mr. Henry Bardiner — the last only of whom is now left.

Mr. Gavin Steele, druggist, had his shop in Chalmers Street, and lived for some time in the same apartments with us in the same street.

Mr. John Miller, Bridge Street, and Messrs. William Clark and James Bonar, High Street, were the principal booksellers.

ANNULAR ECLIPSE OF THE SUN ON 15TH MAY 1836.

There was one great event that took place during my sojourn in Dunfermline, which I think may not be uninteresting to refer to for a little, as the like of it will not be seen in Scotland again for more than a hundred years, and that was an almost total eclipse of the sun. This wonderful phenomenon took place on a Sabbath day, the 15th May 1836, and engrossed the attention of the people far more than the sermons that were preached that day; and, indeed, it was itself a great sermon, as showing how the wonderful works of the Great Creator far transcend any piece of human mechanism and skill, and that the movements of the mighty universe of God are so perfectly controlled by Him, that the time when this eclipse was to begin, and when it was to end, were foretold to a moment, and (although the same event had not happened for nearly two hundred years before) were found to be perfectly correct.

No piece of human clockwork can at all compare to the great clockwork of the heavens, for, although circling through space with inconceivable speed, those mighty worlds by which we are surrounded, and the

one in which we ourselves dwell, never vary in the pre-
cision of their movements by a single hairbreadth, but
are at the appointed spot at the appointed time, guided
by the unerring hand of the Great Jehovah. Our
astronomers, therefore, can say with perfect certainty,
this or that eclipse, or this or that transit of a
planet over the sun's disc, shall begin and end on such
a day, in such an hour, and at such a minute, and
have not the slightest fear of their predictions being
wrong. Watches and clocks may and do vary, but
the clockwork of the heavens, never. Truly we can
say with the Psalmist David, and with much more
emphasis than he (from our more perfect knowledge
of the heavens than existed in his day), 'When we
consider the heavens, the works of Thy hands, the sun,
moon, and stars, which Thou hast ordained; what is
man, that Thou art mindful of him? or the son of man,
that Thou graciously condescendest to visit him?'

What a wonderful body the sun is, which was on this
occasion almost entirely hid from our view—one million
and a quarter times bigger than this world! We can
write it down in figures, but the mind cannot grasp the
idea of such an enormous body, and we wonder how there
can be room in the heavens to contain it. But when
we think that there are hundreds of thousands of such
suns as ours, with worlds, no doubt, revolving around
them, like our own, we are utterly lost in amazement
and overwhelmed with awe, and feel that this little world
of ours—which we used to think so big—is as but a
drop in the ocean of immensity. Yet how cheering it
is to know that the same Creator who formed and upholds this great system of suns and worlds, created and
upholds the smallest animalcule in a drop of water,
and that a sparrow cannot fall to the ground without

His knowledge; and who, moreover, when His creatures
in this world sinned and rebelled against Him, sent His
Son Jesus Christ into it to die for them and atone
for their guilt.   'O the depth of the riches both
of the wisdom and knowledge of God! how unsearch-
able are His judgments, and His ways past finding
out!'

Our moon, during this eclipse, went right over the
centre of the sun; and had it been only a very little
bigger, or a little nearer us, the sun would have been
entirely hid from our view.   Although it was generally
called 'total,' therefore (and it was as nearly so as it
almost ever can be), there was still a streak of light—
like a silver thread—right round the sun, which gave a
very faint glimmer of light; but so faint, that the darkness was very awe-inspiring, and the stars in great
numbers were quite visible.

It was through the kindness of Mrs. Anderson of
Viewfield (a very old friend of my mother's) that I got
into Mr. Inglis's shop, and during my whole three years'
sojourn in Dunfermline received the greatest kindness
from her.   I sat in her seat in the Abbey Church, and
was very frequently in Viewfield.   It was from her
garden I viewed this great eclipse.   Mrs. Wyld, her
only daughter, was then a young lady of great promise,
and much esteemed by every one who knew her.   Mrs.
Anderson died in June 1865, aged eighty-three years,
and was buried in the Abbey churchyard.

During my residence in Dunfermline there were two
public 'characters' who were well known throughout
the whole town—'Daft Archie,' and Bobbie Gow.   We
sometimes used to think that Archie 'was more rogue
than fool.'   He was at times rather violent, and not
one to be much tampered with.   Bobbie, on the other

hand, was a harmless, innocent imbecile, always in a happy mood, and at times very amusing.

Before passing from my sojourn in Dunfermline, it may be interesting to refer to the means of locomotion in those days. The occasional route from Dollar to Dunfermline was to walk to Alloa, get the steamer from there to Charleston, and thence to Dunfermline by a horse railway. But the more frequent route was by Saline on 'Shanks Naigie;' and many is the time I tramped the solitary journey between the two places— distance 12 miles. How different from now-a-days, when we can be whisked about from place to place at the rate of 40 miles an hour, and take journeys of many hundreds of miles without a moment's consideration !

CHAPTER VII.

BEGIN BUSINESS IN DOLLAR.

AFTER finishing my apprenticeship in Dunfermline, I got into Stewart & M'Donald's, Glasgow, and continued there for some little time. This prosperous firm was then doing a very large retail business (their premises being generally crowded every day), and was just creeping into a wholesale one, although no hands were then specially employed for this branch of their business. Mr. Stewart appeared considerably older than Mr. M'Donald, but both were very active and pushing—the latter particularly so. Mr. Hugh Fraser (who afterwards commenced business in company with Mr. Arthur, under the firm of Arthur & Fraser) was one of the principal hands in the establishment, and frequently accompanied Mr. M'Donald to London, Paris, etc., and assisted him in buying. Mr. Byars (who afterwards commenced business in company with Mr. Mann and Mr. Simpson, under the firm of Mann, Simpson, & Byars—now Mann, Byars, & Co.) was at the head of the counting-house; and Mr. Archibald Crombie superintended the execution of all orders that were sent in to the firm. Mr. James Dawson was 'shop-walker;' and Mr. Alexander M'Donald, Mr. Alexander Miller, Mr. Robert Mason, Mr. Brown, Mr. M'Kechnie, Mr. John Innis, and Mr. James Fairlie (of Mr. Girdwood's, Tanfield, Edinburgh), had all charge of important departments.

At the same time that Stewart & M'Donald were pushing such a prosperous business in Buchanan Street, the old-established firm of J. & W. Campbell & Co. had a large retail business in Candleriggs—in addition to their very extensive wholesale one. George Smith & Sons, in London Street, and Wingate, Son, & Co. in Queen Street, were then doing large wholesale businesses.

Mr. James Campbell (of J. & W. Campbell & Co.) was seldom seen in the warehouse, but Mr. William— who was very active and pushing—was constantly moving about through the wholesale departments of their large establishment, and was well known to, and much respected by, every buyer who called. Mr. George Smith (of George Smith & Sons)—although always superintending—left, at that time, the active management of their extensive business to his two sons, who were exceedingly shrewd, pushing business men. Mr. Brock was, for a very long period, one of their much-respected travellers, and was well known throughout all Scotland.

Mr. Andrew Wingate (the senior partner of Wingate, Son, & Co.) was a very worthy old gentleman, and greatly respected in Glasgow. Mr. William Page (brother of Mr. John Page, Alloa) was for a considerable time shawl buyer for this firm, and in that capacity regularly visited 'the hillfoots.' He was a very pushing business young man, of a warm-hearted, genial disposition, and for a number of years mixed a great deal with the society at the foot of the Ochils.

To give an idea how much Glasgow has increased to the west since those days (forty-four years ago), I may mention that Woodside Crescent was then just newly built (if indeed it was quite finished); and between it and the city there were brickworks and sawpits; and, being the only crescent in that quarter, it was always spoken of as 'The Crescent.' Woodlands House stood in the centre of the field which is now the grand West End Park.

After leaving Glasgow, and the prospect being at that time that the New Town of Dollar (as it was called) would by and by become the most important part of the village, my father resolved to build that house and shop at present owned and occupied by Mr. Gibb (which were afterwards largely added to by my brother), and gave up to my brother and me the clothing and drapery part of his business; and in the end of the year 1839 the firm of J. & W. Gibson was started as a drapery establishment, my father continuing the grocery and ironmongery business in the Old Town.

Shortly after we commenced business, we were asked to open a sub-branch, under Tillicoultry, of the Edinburgh and Leith Bank, which continued for a number of years, and ultimately became a branch by itself of the Edinburgh and Glasgow Bank. This was the commencement of that banking business which my brother has now carried on for so long a period, and for the last twenty-five years in connection with the Clydesdale Bank.

SCIENTIFIC DISCOVERIES AND PROGRESS IN THE
NINETEENTH CENTURY.

The present generation can scarcely form a proper idea of the many advantages they enjoy, as compared to the state of matters forty years ago. Gas had not then been introduced into any of the smaller villages of Scotland; and houses and shops had to be content with the dim flicker of the tallow candle (paraffine oil not being then known), requiring 'snuffing' or 'topping' every few minutes all the night over. Now, we have not only gas—that most useful illuminator—but the still more wonderful electric light, which as much casts gas into the shade as gas did the tallow candle. The Dollar gas-work was started in 1845, and my brother was instrumental in getting it up, and for many years took an active part in its management.

When he and I commenced business, it was the days of dear postage (a letter to Glasgow costing 7d., and one to London about 1s. 2d.); and in place of sending our orders to Glasgow through the post office three times a day as at present, we sent them once a week by Robert Young, the Leslie carrier, who, with from eight to ten heavily-laden carts, made the journey from Leslie to Glasgow, and *vice versâ*, once a week, collecting and delivering goods at all the little towns by the way. On reaching Glasgow, he opened the parcel of letters, and delivered them to the different parties to whom they were addressed. Now we have the 'one ounce' letter for a penny, and the halfpenny post card, which have proved such an inestimable boon to the country, and facilitated business to an extent that the present generation can scarcely conceive of. And we are not content with this only, but must have our orders and communications flashed through the electric wire with lightning speed, and think less of the expense of a telegram now than we used to do in days of old of a letter that took days for its journey by the lumbering old mail coach.

The electric telegraph is truly one of the greatest discoveries of the age, and will for ever make the nineteenth century memorable. It really seems fabulous that events that happened in America, and indeed in almost any part of the world, yesterday, can be published in to-day's newspapers! Yet so it is; for, scorning the dangers of the mighty depths of the ocean, the electric current speeds along as quickly at the bottom of the great world of waters as it does above ground, and binds the different nations of the earth together as with a magic band.

On the 17th of August 1858, the extremities of the *first* Atlantic cable were put in connection with the recording instruments, and the following message was flashed through the ocean: 'Europe and America are united by telegraph. Glory to God in the highest; on earth peace, and good-will towards men.'

Electricity is now being largely used, also, as a motive-power on short lines of railways, and for other purposes; and, where water-power can be made available for generating the electricity, is one of the cheapest motive-powers that has yet been discovered. The most wonderful thing regarding it is that it can be stored, and made available long after it has been generated.

Then we have got recently introduced that most scientific discovery, the telephone, by which we can talk to each other through a wire, when far separated from one another; and thus business people save an immense amount of time and shoe leather. Place one of our forefathers in some of the principal streets of any of our great cities,—say at the Exchange, or in Queen Street, Glasgow,—and make him look up, and what would be his surprise to see a very network of wires stretching in all directions, and so close in

some places that the very birds will have some difficulty in flying through them. Then what are all these
for ? How astonished would he be when told, they
were to enable the inhabitants of the great city,
although miles apart, to talk to each other through the
telephone office, and thus save an untold amount of
time and running hither and thither to see each other.
But how wide would he open his eyes when told that
not only can this be done, but that talking goes on
through it between places at great distances from each
other, and that business transactions between Glasgow
and Greenock are regularly carried on by means of it.
The services of the sanctuary, also, can be enjoyed by
invalids in their beds, at great distances away from
church, through this great discovery ; and our worthy
townsman, James Paton, Esq., Tillicoultry, has for the
last twelvemonth been indebted to it for hearing all
the services in the U.P. Church ; and a whisper, or
even a loud sigh, can be heard distinctly through it.
The singing of the choir, too, with all the different
parts, is distinctly heard.

In an article published recently on ' Progress in
Telephony,' some most interesting statements are given
of the rapid progress that has been made, and I think
I cannot do better than give a few extracts from it
here. It says : ' No invention of modern times took
the public more by surprise than did the telephone, a
result due not more to the marvellousness of the thing
done—namely, the transmission of spoken words along
a telegraph wire—than to the simplicity of the means
by which it was accomplished. Seldom, also, has an
invention given rise so soon to an important industry.
Five years ago, the telephone was being viewed by the
savants of the British Association with the interest

attaching to the very latest novelty in scientific toys; it is now, according to Mr. Preece of the Telegraph Department, employing in the United Kingdom alone more than a million and a half sterling of capital, and earning over £100,000 in dividends. The practical instrument of to-day, however, differs considerably from the scientific toy patented about six years ago by Professor Bell.' After describing the construction of the instrument, and the various improvements made on it by different scientific men, it continues : ' Conversation has been carried on by telephone over a distance of 500 miles in India, and over 410 miles in America; and Mr. Preece states that if a wire were placed on lofty poles, and away from all other wires, between John-o'-Groat's and Land's End, there would be no difficulty in speaking between those two places. . . . . Already the telephone exchange system is being worked in almost all the principal cities and towns of Europe and America. Paris has its central exchange, with nearly a thousand wires converging upon it, besides several branch exchanges connected with the central one. The Parisians avoid the unsightliness and danger of a great network of overground wires, however, by placing the telephone wires in the sewers. . . . . Nowhere is the system better organized than in Berlin, where there are four exchanges, besides two public telephone offices, in which any person, on payment of sixpence, is permitted to have five minutes' conversation with any one whose house is connected with the central office. . . . . In New York alone there are thirteen exchanges, with over 5000 subscribers, besides 1500 private telephone wires. The use to which those exchanges may be put need not be confined merely to enabling subscribers to converse with each other, and already many other purposes are being found for them. Thus, according to Colonel Webber, in a recent paper on the subject, subscribers can arrange to be wakened by the exchange ringing their bell at any appointed hour ; and correct time, say at noon, might be sent on all subscribers' wires by the striking of a public clock heard simultaneously on every telephone on the system. In the New York prisons transmitting telephones are placed in the cell walls, from which wires are led to receivers in another part of the building, and important conversations between prisoners have, it is said, been thus heard, which have materially assisted the ends of justice.'

With the aid of a newly-patented wire, experiments were recently made with the telephone between New York and Chicago (1000 miles apart), which proved entirely successful—a conversation being carried on between those two far - distant places ! This is certainly the crowning triumph of this wonderful discovery.

It is contemplated, I understand, to introduce *penny* telephone messages into London ; and if this is carried out, it will likely be extended over the whole kingdom. People will then be able to carry on a conversation between ' Land's End ' and ' John-o'-Groat's House ' for the small charge of one penny.

What wonderful discoveries have been made in our day in chemistry, geology, astronomy, etc. ! Notably among the first of these may be specified the beautiful aniline dyes we are now possessed of, which have so thoroughly superseded a great many of our old dingy-looking colours, and which, from their gorgeous brilliancy, have added so much to the beauty of all our textile fabrics. Chemical science has given us these, and principally from an article that was at one time looked upon as of little value, and for which it was difficult to find any use, viz. coal tar. Then, in geology, what wonderful revelations have been made to us of the age of our world by Hugh Miller and other scientific men. In astronomy, every increased power of the telescope has revealed to us greater and greater wonders, and given us such glimpses into the mighty universe of God, that the mind is overwhelmed with awe. In art, those beautiful oleograph pictures we now possess are of but very recent date, and furnish another proof of the scientific skill of the present day. When we are told that in some of those pictures as many as sixteen colours require to be printed, separately, ere the picture is finished, it will be seen at once with what scientific skill the machines on which they are produced must be constructed. Then photography is one of the great discoveries of this century, which has enabled people in humble circumstances in life to get portraits of themselves and their friends, who could not otherwise have possibly obtained them. It was unknown in my young days, and the first portrait (or profile, rather) I ever got taken of myself was done by a machine, was painted black, and had golden hair put in!

The first time I went to London by land (about 1841), there was no railway beyond Lancaster, and I had to 'coach it' from Edinburgh (by Hawick, Langholm, Carlisle, and Kendal) to Lancaster; and from thence to London by rail, taking part of two days and two nights for the journey, and costing between £5 and £6. Now the journey can be accomplished in ten hours, and a return ticket from Edinburgh got for about £2, 10s.

Before the Edinburgh and Glasgow Railway was made, we had to walk to Alloa, and get the 'Earl of Mar' coach from there to Glasgow, taking five hours on the road. The coaches entered the city by Duke Street, High Street, and drew up at Mein's Hotel in the Trongate, a little to the west of the Tron Church, and on the opposite side of the street. After the Edinburgh and Glasgow line was opened (in 1842), an omnibus was started from Tillicoultry to Stirling (with Hugh Black for driver), and we got the coach (driven by Lowrie M'Laren) from there to Castlecary Station ; and from Alloa the coach ran, by way of Dunmore, Airth, and Carron, to Falkirk Station. Thus gradually the benefits of railway travelling were approaching nearer us. When the Scottish Central line from Greenhill to Perth was opened (in 1848), the journey from Stirling to Edinburgh or Glasgow could be accomplished all the way by rail. Afterwards the Stirling and Dunfermline line was made, and then the Devon Valley ; and thus the great iron roads which we now possess were gradually introduced into Scotland, and the old mode of travelling by the stage-coach done away with.

The portion of the Stirling and Dunfermline line from Alloa to Dunfermline was opened in 1850 ; from Alloa to Stirling and Tillicoultry in 1852. On the Devon Valley route, the portion from Kinross to Rumbling Bridge was opened in 1862 ; from Tillicoultry to Dollar, in 1869 ; and the connecting link between Dollar and Rumbling Bridge (thus completing the railway), in 1871.

The present generation can scarcely conceive of the dread with which people looked on a journey by rail when railways were first introduced, and many of the old folks wouldn't think of such a thing. My worthy old aunt of Clackmannan used to say ' it was a tempting of Providence ' to go into a train, and she never did, although she lived long after they were introduced.

Drawn & Eng.ᵈ By W. Banks, Edin.

RUMBLING BRIDGE.

This same aunt used to tell me that in her young days she walked all the way from Clackmannan to Paisley to see her brother; but after the Forth and Clyde Canal was constructed, she walked to Lock 16, and got the canal boat there.

I recollect well of another old lady friend of mine, who was going from Edinburgh to Glasgow shortly after the railway between those two places was opened, and I urged her strongly, of course, to go by rail; but no, she was sure to be killed if she hazarded her life on any such perilous undertaking, and so, clinging to her old notions of things (like so many old folks), she went by the canal boat, taking some ten hours by the way, and passing through who knows how many locks.

We cannot now appreciate too highly the immense strides the press has taken since those early days, and the great social, political, and religious advantages we derive from the cheap and excellent literature of the present day. Those charming pictorial books that are now produced every year in such profusion for the children, were unknown fifty years ago; and who can estimate the advantage this is to a rising generation? Then the beautifully-illustrated school-books we now possess, and the interesting and instructive matter of which they are generally composed, give an interest to the scholars in their lessons that didn't exist formerly, and must tend greatly to forward the education of the young. In the matter of cheapness, also, it seems perfectly fabulous the prices at which books can now be published, as compared to the early times of which I have been writing. The first Testament I ever possessed cost 3s. 6d.; and just think of getting one now for 3d.!

But dear as my Testament was, what would one have

K

cost before the art of printing was discovered at all? The town of Mayence on the Rhine has the honour of being the birthplace of the genius who made this invaluable discovery. John Gutenberg showed his first printed sheets to Faust in 1448; and the first book (supposed to be a Bible) was printed in 1450.

A heavy duty existed in my young days on paper, and the Government imposed a heavy tax on newspapers; and instead of getting our morning and evening papers, as we do now, for the small sum of a penny and halfpenny, a club of half a dozen or so got a newspaper once a week among them—costing 7d.; and each got a reading of it, for a few hours, in his turn. I remember well of my father being a member of such a club. When the Government removed both duties, the press, being freed from such unnatural shackles, took a bound in the way of progress that seems now perfectly fabulous. This is seen specially in the charming illustrated weekly newspapers that are now published, such as the *Graphic, Illustrated London News,* etc., where, for the small charge of sixpence, you can get as many really highly artistic engravings as would have cost pounds sterling in days of old, and, in addition, all the general news of the week. Our advantages now are unspeakably great, and our responsibilities in consequence immensely increased, and it would be well that we should all feel this, and act accordingly.

While the press is powerful for good, it is also powerful for evil, when the streams which flow from it are polluted; and it is very much to be regretted that at the present day such an amount of pernicious literature is constantly making its appearance, and poisoning the minds of all who read it. Parents, therefore, cannot be too careful what sort of books they allow their children to get into their hands, and should exercise the strictest scrutiny in this respect.

Truly it has been my lot to live in the age of the greatest discoveries in the arts and sciences of any period of our globe's history, and our advantages now are very great indeed. I often wonder how we got on at all in those early times, and how business was ever managed. But, knowing no better, we jogged along somehow, and people contrived to make money then as they do now, and seemed to enjoy the comforts of life as much as at the present day.

ESTABLISHED CHURCH OF DOLLAR AND FREE CHURCH AT SHELTERHALL.

It was during my partnership with my brother that the building of the present Established Church of Dollar was commenced (about the year 1840), and I used frequently to go up and inspect the operations as they were going on.

The feuars of Dollar were very indignant at being brought in by the heritors to pay a share of this new church—a thing that had been almost unheard-of till then; and my father (from being possessed of a good deal of heritable property) had a pretty large sum to pay. He, however, got in consequence a very nice seat allocated to him in the new building; but the Disruption coming on very soon after (in 1843), he didn't enjoy it long, for, casting in his lot with the Free Church, he joined the church that was built at Shelterhall, and left the Church of his fathers. This church at Shelterhall was a plain one-storied building, with a slated roof, and was built at Shelterhall, as being about half-way between Muckart and Dollar, so as to accommodate both places. The Rev. James Thomson of Muckart was chosen as the first minister of this joint congregation. It was found, however, to be very inconvenient to have to go so far to church, particularly in winter, and ultimately a church was built in Dollar for the inhabitants of Dollar alone—the folks in Muckart having either to go back to the Established Church, join the U.P. one, or go to Fossoway Free Church. Mr. Thomson married Miss Monteath of Dollarbank, who was cut off in the prime of life, and was interred in Tillicoultry Cemetery in May 1867. Mr. Thomson died in Edinburgh, and was buried there in December 1871, aged seventy-one years.

MILNATHORT—'COACHING DAYS,' ETC.

After nearly a four years' copartnery with my brother in Dollar, I left in 1843, to commence business in Milnathort, where I continued for four years. While there I attended the ministry of the Rev. James Thornton of the Free Church. I boarded, during my sojourn there, with Mrs. Mitchell, Mr. Thornton's sister, then a widow with a large young family. The Rev. Mr. Little was then (and still is) minister of the Established, and the Rev. Mr. Leslie of the U.P. Church.

The Rev. James Hay, D.D., and the Rev. Robert Leishman, were ministers of the two U.P. Churches in Kinross; the Rev. John Wright was (and is still) minister of the Free Church; and the Rev. William Peters was (and still continues) minister of the Established Church. The Rev. Dr. Hay died 14th June 1849.

Mr. Shaw and Mr. David Reddie were the only drapers in Milnathort when I went there; and the principal ones in Kinross were Mr. John Brough and Mr. Thomas Crooks. The most extensive grocery businesses in Kinross were those of Mr. Joseph Hardie (afterwards Mr. David Sands), Mr. Hutton, and Mr. Steedman.

Mr. Williamson and Mr. Hugh Laird were the principal writers and bankers; and Dr. Annan and Dr. Gray were the two medical men in Kinross. The two doctors in Milnathort were Dr. Roy and Dr. Lilburn. Mr. George Barnet was (and still is) the only printer and publisher in the county town of Kinross.

I may here give the names of a few of the gentlemen in the town and neighbourhood of Milnathort :—

Mr. Charles Stein, Hattonburn.
Mr. G. Walker Arnot, Arlary.
Mr. Andrew Boosie, Burleigh.
Mr. David Tod, Collinton.
Mr. William Tod, Gospetry.
Mr. George Tod, Lochran.
Mr. James Simpson, Mawcarse.
Captain Wilson, Orwell.
Mr. John Laing, Balgedie.
Rev. Dr. M'Kelvie, Balgedie.
Mr. Thomas Stobie, Balnethal.
Mr. John Beveridge, Kinneston.
Mr. Robert Reid, Tilliery.
Mr. John Black, Tilliewhally.
Mr. David Greig, Tilliery.
Mr. Robert Nelson, Hilton.
Mr James Robertson, Teuchie.
Mr. John Ewing, Shanwell and Hattonburn.

Mr. Andrew Reddie, Netherhall.
Mr. John Reddie, Cuthil.
Mr. James Hutton, Waulkmill and Ballingall.
Mr. John Horn, Thomanane.
Mr. James Archibald, Mawhill.
Dr. Young, Hallhill.
Mr. James Dempster, Tillyochie.
Mr. John Henderson, Turfhills.
Mr. James Beveridge, Balado.
Mr. Coventry, Coldrain.
Rev. James Cullen, Free Church Minister, Kelty.
Mr. Alexander Forfar, Milnathort.
Mr. Hugh Forfar, Milnathort.
Mr. David Thomson, Milnathort.
Mr. Whyte, Milnathort.
Mr. Greig, Lethangie.
Mr. John Sands, Kinross.

The tartan manufacture was at that time in a very flourishing condition in Milnathort and Kinross, and gave employment to a great many hands. The principal manufacturers in Milnathort were :—

| Messrs. Wittet & Chapman. | Mr. John Wright. |
| Mr. Robert Henderson. | Mr. Robert Gordon. |

In Kinross :—

Messrs. Andrew Thomson & Co.	Mr. Thomas Marshall.
,, Wm. & Robt. Beveridge.	,, David Arnot.
Mr. Robert Watson.	,, William Watson.
,, David Whyte.	,, John Deas.
,. Robert Whyte.	

The only two firms now in the trade are Messrs.
Wittet & Chapman in Milnathort, and W. & R.
Beveridge in Kinross.   Mr. Stark now carries on the
business of Wittet & Chapman, and two sons of Mr.
William Beveridge that of W. & R. Beveridge.   The
only survivors of the original foregoing firms are Mr.
Michael Chapman and Mr. Robert Gordon, neither of
whom is now in the trade.   My good and worthy
minister, the Rev. James Thornton, died on 3d September 1874.

One of my old apprentices (Mr. John Hogg, a native
of Milnathort) has been long at the head of one of the
largest drapery establishments in Boston, America; and
Mr. George Hutton was another of my apprentices while
in Milnathort.   Mr. Thomas Forbes, Kinross, and Mr.
John Henderson (afterwards of the Castle Campbell
Hotel, Dollar) were also with me for some time.

There was rather an eccentric blacksmith in Milnathort in those days, and his signboard caused great
amusement to strangers when passing.   It was as
follows :—

> ' Tammie Wallace, jobbing smith,
> Works up this close wi' a' his pith ;
> He'll dae yer job baith neat and sune,
> And hopes ye'll pay whene'er it's dune. '

Milnathort being situated on the Great North Road

which runs from Land's End to John-o'-Groat's House,
the amount of traffic that passed through it at certain
seasons of the year was very great indeed. There were
four public conveyances between Edinburgh and Perth
each way daily—the Mail and 'Defiance' stage-coaches ;
and the number of gentlemen's carriages when the
shooting season approached was something fabulous.
It was said that at Mr. Mitchell's hotel and posting
establishment at North Queensferry about one hundred
horses were regularly kept; and the number at Kirkland's hotel, Kinross, would, I suppose, be about the
same—as fresh horses were regularly got at Kinross.
When the Edinburgh, Perth, and Dundee Railway
through Fife was opened (in 1848), all this was entirely
changed ; and where all was stir and bustle before,
something like a deathlike silence at once took its place.
In this way the introduction of railways suddenly
changed many bustling country towns and villages
throughout the kingdom into quiet, rural, deserted-
looking places, and completely ruined many prosperous
hotels.

In 1846 my father paid me a visit in Milnathort,
and remained with me for some days, and although not
feeling quite well, was not much out of his usual. On
his return to Dollar (on a Thursday, I think it was) I
walked with him the length of Thomanane, and there
bade him good-bye—a last good-bye, as it turned out to
be, in this world, for on the Monday morning following, a conveyance came for me from Dollar, with the sad
news that my father had taken suddenly and seriously
ill on coming home from church on Sabbath-day, and
was no better. When nearing Dollar, George Tod met
and told me that all was over—that my father was gone,
cut off after a few hours' illness. Thus, at the comparat-

ively early age of fifty-seven, I lost my good and worthy father—taken suddenly away in the midst of his usefulness, and leaving my three young sisters alone in the old home.

The manufacturing trade at the foot of the Ochils being very good at that time, I was induced to leave my old business, and left Milnathort for Tillicoultry in the year 1847. Through the kindness of my brother-in-law, Mr. Robert Archibald, of Devonvale, I learned some of the branches of manufacturing, and commenced business on my own account in 1848; and now for thirty-five years I have been engaged in wool spinning and manufacturing. In 1851 my brother-in-law and I entered into partnership, and under the firm of William Gibson & Co. carried on business together for nineteen years, in Craigfoot and Dawson's Mills. In 1870 Mr. Archibald left the business, and I then carried it on for some years by myself, and since then in partnership with my eldest son, under the same old firm.

CHAPTER VIII.

IT may not be uninteresting here to say a few words about the town and trade of Tillicoultry, which has now for so long a period been the place of my abode.

There is an old story told of how Tillicoultry got its name, and it really has 'the ring' of probability about it. A Highlandman was taking a drove of cattle along the old road, and when passing through Tillicoultry Burn, none of the cattle took a drink, when, in astonishment, he exclaimed, 'There's Tiel a coo try' (Deil a cow dry), in Tonald's way of pronouncing the D; and hence the town, it is said, got its name. However, the writers of both the Statistical Accounts of Scotland say that the etymology of the word is purely Celtic, and is composed of three words—*Tullich-Cul-tir*, and signifies 'The mount or hill at the back of the country;' or, as a Gaelic correspondent puts it, 'The hill behind the stretch of land.' The Rev. William Osborn (the writer of the first Statistical Account) suggests the possibility of the name being derived from the Latin words *Tellus culta*, 'The cultivated land.'

We learn from that interesting little book, *Tillicoultry in Olden Times* (by Mr. Watson, headmaster of our public school here, and published by Mr. Roxburgh of the *Tillicoultry News* office, price sixpence), that the estate of Tillicoultry was granted to the family of Mar in 1261, the fourteenth year of the reign of Alexander the Third ; and from that very early date to the present day it has passed through the hands of no fewer than eleven proprietors,—Lord Colville of Culross and the Earl of Stirling being amongst the number,—until in 1814 it came into the hands of R. Wardlaw Ramsay, Esq., the father of the present proprietor, and in 1840 into the possession of his son, the present laird—Robert Balfour Wardlaw Ramsay, Esq., who is also proprietor of the fine estate of Whitehill, near Edinburgh.

The Kirk Hill, or Cunninghar Hill, which begins at the Devon, and goes up to near Tillicoultry House, and on the south end of which our beautiful cemetery has been formed, is, to the antiquarian, the most interesting part of the estate.   Immediately opposite the cemetery lodge, on the north side of the public road, and close to it, a large portion of a druidical circle can still be seen, of about 130 feet in diameter, which (but for the Vandalism of some modern builder, as Mr. Watson informs us) might have been one of the most interesting sights in Scotland.   A number of old druidical stones, five and a half feet high, stood at one time in the circle, but by this Goth of a fellow had been removed (very probably to build a dyke with).   Had these still remained, the true nature of the place would have been apparent at a glance.   Now, however, it is difficult to tell what it has been ; and but for the old Statistical Account of Scotland (from which Mr. Watson got his information), people would have been a little incredulous as to the true nature of the place.

The same Vandalism is—in this nineteenth century of ours—still going on ; for this famous old relic of antiquity is being gradually carted away in the shape of sand—the one half of it having already disappeared into the great sand-pit adjoining. Had the present proprietor resided at Tillicoultry instead of Whitehill, this surely would never have been allowed to go on.

From several urns containing human bones having been dug up at the north end of the Cunninghar Hill, it is supposed the Romans had a station here; and an old rusty sword, evidently of Roman make, was dug up a little farther east, near to Harviestoun Castle.

In early days there were three villages in the parish of Tillicoultry—Eastertown, Westertown, and Coalsnaughton. Harvieston Burn ran through the centre of Eastertown; and that portion of the village on the west side of the burn was called Ellieston, while that on the east side was called Harviestoun. It was situated above the present road on the north side of the Castle, and close to where the home farm now is. It was, in early times, larger than Westertown, although not a vestige of it now remains. It was entirely removed by Mr. Tait when he formed the garden for Harviestoun Castle, on the site of which it stood. The road from Eastertown to Dollar was by Whitehillhead, and joining the old highway at the villa of Belmont. Mr. Andrew Rutherford, of the post office, Dollar, is a native of Ellieston, and attended the school in Tillicoultry when a boy.

Tillicoultry—as at present—is Westertown very much enlarged; and the old church, manse, and churchyard were situated between the two, close to Tillicoultry House. The first manse on the present site was built in 1730; the first church on the present site in 1773; and the present handsome building in 1829.

A curious legend is told about the old churchyard of Tillicoultry, which is situated at the back of the mansion house. A wicked laird quarrelled with one of the

monks of Cambuskenneth, and in the heat and excitement of the moment actually knocked the holy father
down. Dying shortly after this, it was discovered next
morning after the funeral, that the wicked clenched fist
that dealt the sacrilegious blow was projecting out of the
grave, and it was looked upon as a punishment sent upon
him from heaven for his wicked conduct. However, as
this couldn't be allowed to remain, the grave was opened
and the hand replaced in it, and an end, it was thought,
put to the dreadful apparition. What, then, was the
good folks' surprise, on paying a visit to the grave on
the following morning, to find the terrible hand up again.
This was repeated day after day for a whole week, till
the people were getting into an alarming state of excitement and terror. As a last resource, however, an
immense stone was brought and placed over the grave,
and now the hand no longer appeared. This stone was
too heavy for the monks to roll away, and repeat the
imposition they had evidently been practising upon these
simple-minded and superstitious folks; and hence the
hand now got rest. This legend gave rise to the old
Scotch saying, when any one had given a blow, 'Your
hand 'll wag abune the grave for this yet.' This big
stone, which proved ' *one too many* ' for the monks, is still
pointed out in the old churchyard. (For other information about Tillicoultry in days of old, see Mr. Watson's
very interesting little book.)

The population of Tillicoultry parish was—

In 1755,	. . . .	787
„ 1801,	. . . .	916
„ 1837,	. . . .	1803
„ 1851,	. . . .	4686
„ 1881,	. . . .	5544

On the west side of the burn, and overtopping the

village, stands the beautiful Castle Craig, wooded to
the top, and on which stood, in ancient times, a round
Pictish fortress, the traces of which can still be distinctly
seen. This craig is, I think, one of the most picturesque
objects on the Alva estate, and it is a very great pity
that it should be so disfigured by the extensive quarry-
ing operations that are being at present carried on at it.
Not far from the foot of this craig, and on the same site
where Castle Mills dwelling-house now stands, an old
castle stood, in the beginning of this century, inhabited
by two old maiden ladies—Misses Kirkwood—of whom
Mr. Edward Moir has a distinct recollection. It was
afterwards occupied by one Thomas Harrower, who
manufactured ' a drop of the cratur ' on his own account;
and the excise officers, getting to hear of this, surrounded
the castle, and summoned Thomas to surrender; but he
was deaf to all entreaties, and would not open the great
old door (full of large-headed nails) to them. Recourse
was then had, therefore, to force, and a supply of large
forehammers procured from a smithy down the village,
and with these the big old door was soon hammered to
pieces, the sound of the knocks being distinctly heard
in Mr. Moir's dwelling-house, a long way from the
castle. It would be either from this old castle, or the
Pictish fortress on the top of the craig, that Castle Craig
got its name; but from which, it is not easy now to say.
A little below this castle, a meal-mill was carried on in
those days by a man named William Carmichael, but it
has long since entirely disappeared. Its site was where
the entrance gate now is.

About twenty-five years ago, the damhead or reservoir
for the public works of Tillicoultry (erected in 1824)
stood a little above the quarry, at the very mouth of the
glen; but as it was getting old, and a new one required,

a much more suitable site was fixed on for it, about a quarter of a mile back the glen, and the present dam-head was then built. Our late worthy townsman, Mr. Graham Paterson, was the architect and builder of it, and a most substantial job he made of it. The getting up of the enormous logs required in its construction proved a very formidable undertaking, and attracted a great amount of attention and curiosity. A carriage had to be specially made for the purpose, and on it they were dragged up the sledge road, entering by the gate near the Wood Burn, a number of horses being required in the operation. It was erected in 1853–1854, and cost £515.

The damhead is situated in a very romantic part of the glen, and is well worthy of a visit. Indeed, the whole glen, up to the base of Ben Cleugh, is rocky, precipitous, and wild, and would quite compare with some of the finest Highland scenery, and one could almost imagine himself in the midst of the Grampians. The hills immediately behind Tillicoultry are—the Miller Hill, to the west of the burn ; adjoining it, on the west, is the beautiful Wood Hill, on which the mansion-house of James Johnston, Esq. of Alva, stands ; the Law, between the two branches of Tillicoultry Burn ; Ben Cleugh (the highest hill of the Ochil range—2363 feet high) is immediately behind the Law ; the Whum and Andrew Ganhill are to the east of the Law ; and imme-diately beyond them is Maddy-Moss. The hill above Tillicoultry, on the east side of the burn, is called Tillicoultry Hill. The one between Tillicoultry House Burn (or 'Back Burn ') and Harviestoun Burn, is Ellieston Hill—the east half of which is in Harviestoun estate, and the west half in that of Tillicoultry—the stone dyke which separates the two properties running up the centre of it. The hills on the east side of Harviestoun Burn are, the Grains Hill, Harviestoun Hill, and Dollar Bank Hill — all three terminating in the farther back and second highest peak of the Ochils, the King's Seat.

Tillicoultry Burn, and the other streams of the Ochils utilized for water-power, have been rendered of very much less value to the millowners than they used to be, from the extensive system of drainage that has been carried on for the last thirty years all over the Ochil range. Previous to this, the extensive morasses that exist on the hills used to act as natural reservoirs; and after a heavy rain, good full water was experienced for several weeks. Now, with the deep drains that intersect these places in all directions, the greater part of the water rushes off as fast as it falls, and in two or three days after a flood the streams are as small as ever. In consequence of this, the water-power of our burns has become of very little value indeed, and but for the aid of steam we would be helpless. Helen's Muir, on the back of Tillicoultry Hill, is a fine example of this extensive system of drainage—some of the main drains being of great depth and very wide.

The wire fence that separates the Alva from the Tillicoultry estates runs right up the centre of the Law, and passes within a few feet of the cairn of stones on the top of it; whilst that which separates Tillicoultry from Harviestoun estates, runs up Harviestoun Glen; and both join the one from Maddy-Moss to Ben Cleugh, which is the southern boundary of Back Hill farm. The top and south side of Ben Cleugh are in Alva estate; part of the Law, the Whum, and Andrew Ganhill, are in Tillicoultry estate; while the King's Seat is in Harviestoun estate. Back Hill farm—which extends back to

Devon, with Broich for its eastern boundary, and Green-horn for its western—is in Tillicoultry estate.

On a clear day, the view from the top of Ben Cleugh is very grand, embracing as it does not only the wide Ochil range, stretching in all directions a long way below you, but an extensive view also of Strathearn and the hills beyond Crieff; while to the south, the river Forth, with all the beautiful scenery surrounding it, forms one of the finest panoramas that could be seen anywhere, perhaps, in the British Isles. Benlomond and all the western hills are embraced in the beautiful prospect; while away to the east, the Bass Rock and the mouth of the Firth of Forth can be distinctly seen. The view from Craigleith Hill above Alva, and from Damyat to the west of Menstrie, is also very fine. The latter stands out a little from the rest of the range, and commands a beautiful view of the Devon valley.

The Abbey Craig, on which the Wallace Monument stands, is a rocky spur of the Ochils, and is situated between Logie and Bridge of Allan, and stands out a good way in front of the range. No finer situation could have been selected for this monument to our old Scottish hero, as it is seen from a very great distance in all directions.

From the remains of old turf walls and stone dykes that cover the Ochils in our neighbourhood, it seems very clear that they were at one time possessed by a great many proprietors, and not, as at present, in the hands of two or three. One of these turf walls can be seen, extending from the Mill Glen House to the Wood Burn, and going right over the top of the Miller Hill. That patches of the very tops of the hills, also, had been at one time under the plough, can be distinctly seen on the level plateau on the top of this hill, the deep

Drawn & Engd by W.Banks & Son Edin.r

THE WALLACE MONUMENT

Abbey Craig.

furrows being quite visible from one side of it to the other.

In the end of last century, a Mr. John Cairns (the late Laird Cairns' grandfather) lived in this Mill Glen House, where there had been a considerable sized farm-steading—the foundations of the houses being still distinctly seen, and the form of the garden easily traced. The sledge road would be made for the use of the dwellers in this hill farm. The burn that runs past this house was then called Tankley Burn, but it now generally gets the name of the Mill Glen House Burn. Mr. Edward Moir has a distinct recollection of the last inhabitant of this house ; but he had left it before his day, and was residing in Tillicoultry.

In the old Statistical Account of Tillicoultry, Mr. Osborne says : ' There are many veins of copper in the hills. Some of these were wrought near fifty years ago (about the years 1740 to 1745) to a very considerable extent in the Mill Glen. Four different kinds of copper ore were discovered, the thickest vein of which was about 18 inches. The ore, when washed and dressed, was valued at £50 sterling per ton. A company of gentlemen in London were the tacksmen, and for several years employed about fifty men. After a very great sum of money was expended, the works were abandoned, as unable to defray the expense. Ironstone, of an exceeding good quality, has been found in many different places. Some veins in Watty-Glen are as rich as any discovered in Scotland. Besides copper, there is a great appearance in the hills of different minerals, such as silver, lead, cobalt, antimony, sulphur, and arsenic, but no proper trials have yet been made.'

' The whole parish, south of the hills, abounds with coal. . . . There are four different seams. The first,

L

3 feet thick, 12 fathoms from the surface.   The second,
6 feet thick, 15 fathoms deep.   The third, 2½ feet thick,
20 fathoms deep; and the fourth is about 5 feet
thick, and 30 fathoms deep.'

Mr. Watson, in his interesting little book, says : ' On
the west side of the Mill-Glen are hard grey basaltic
rocks, and on the east side, a species of red granite
capable of taking a polish. . . . The presence of silver
in the Ochils is well known from the history of the
famous silver mine on the Alva estate, from which for
thirteen or fourteen weeks ore to the value of £4000
per week was extracted by the proprietor, Sir John
Erskine of Alva.'   The glen where this mine was
situated still goes by the name of the Silver Glen.   It is
right above Burnside of Alva.

The late Robert Bald, Esq., of Alloa, in his valuable
contribution on ' Geology and Mineralogy,' to the
Statistical Account of Alloa Parish in 1840, says in
regard to the collieries : ' The coals of this parish have
been wrought for a long period of years, but at what
time they commenced is quite uncertain.   It would
appear, however, from some very old papers in possession
of the family of Mar, that coals were wrought previous
to the year 1650 by day-levels.

' The stratification has been satisfactorily proved to the
depth of 140 fathoms, extending beyond the lowest workable seam of coal in the field. . . . The number of seams
of coal found in the depth of 115 fathoms is twenty-one,
the aggregate thickness of which is fully 60 feet.   At
the present time, no coal here is reckoned workable to
profit below 2½ feet thick.   If all the coals below that
thickness are deducted, there remain nine workable coals,
the thinnest of which is 2 feet 8 inches thick, and from
that to 9 feet. . . . Of the thin coals in this parish

some of them are only an inch or two thick. . . . Until
within these thirty years, all the coals in this parish
were brought from the wall face or foreheads of the
mines by women, married and unmarried, old and young;
these were known by the name of bearers. When the
pit was deep, they brought the coals to the pit-bottom;
but when the pits did not exceed 18 fathoms, they
carried the coals to the bank at the pit-head by a stair.
A stout woman carried in general from one hundred
to two hundredweight, and, in a trial of strength,
three hundredweight imperial.'

'As the collieries in this parish extended, this oppressive slavery became evidently worse, and the late most
worthy and excellent John Francis, Earl of Mar, with a
benevolence and philanthropy which does honour to his
memory, ordered this system to be completely abolished.
The evils attending this system may in some degree be
estimated, when it is stated that, when his lordship put
an end to it, 50,000 tons of coals were raised at his
collieries annually, every ounce of which was carried by
women.'

This system of carrying the coals was still in existence
at Dollar in my young days, for I recollect well of
watching the poor women toiling up the long stairs with
their heavy loads. The creels were placed on their
backs, and were supported by a belt put round their
foreheads, and in this way they laboured up the long
stairs of 108 feet (18 fathoms) with their grievous loads
of two and three hundredweights. Truly, as Mr. Bald
says in another place, ' of all the slavery under heaven's
canopy (the African slavery as it was in the West
Indies excepted), this was the most cruel and oppressive.'

No range of hills in Scotland, I believe, possesses a
greater number of fine trout-fishing streams than the

Ochils. I will refer first to that one with which I was earliest acquainted—Dollar Burn. Fine trout used to be got in it (and, I suppose, will still be) from where it falls into the Devon, up to near the very top of its two branches—the Bank and Turnpike Burns. From the upper bridge to a little above the Black Linn, I knew at one time every stream and pool, and almost every stone in it, and fished this part of the burn every other night —the fishing-rod and bait being kept always ready. Considering the number of boys that fished this part of the stream almost every night in the fishing season, it does seem really surprising how a single trout was left in it ; but there they constantly were, and we seldom had to go unrewarded. The great flood of 1877 has entirely swept away all the old landmarks (or rather watermarks) of this part of the burn ; and now the pools and streams which I used to know so well are all entirely gone. An island which existed just below the wood is now joined to the west side of the burn—the branch of the burn which formed it (and in which were some fine fishing pools) being now quite filled up.

The largest and best fishing stream of the Ochils is, of course, the Devon ; to which all the others on the south side of the range, west of Muckart, are tributaries. Rising in the midst of the Ochils, on the back of Craighorn Hill, right north from Alva, the Devon falls into the Forth at Cambus, only a few miles from its source, after a run of about thirty miles. Its course till it reaches Kameknowe is almost due east ; it then turns southwards, and, passing through Glendevon, runs almost due south till it comes to the Crook of Devon (or, ' The Crook,' as it is generally called), where, turning sharply round, it then runs straight west till it passes Menstrie ; and after a short run southwards again, it joins our noble river, the Forth, at Cambus. From Back Hill House to Dollar, no finer trout-fishing ground could be found anywhere than on the Devon. The fine scenery on this stream at Glendevon, the Black Linn, the Rumbling Bridge, and Caldron Linn, is so well known, I will not attempt to describe it. I would merely say to all those who have not seen those celebrated places, they should embrace the first opportunity that comes in their way of doing so, and I am sure they will not be disappointed.

The farthest-up tributary of the Devon that I have fished is the Greenhorn, which rises on the west shoulder of Ben Cleugh, and runs northwards (passing Alva Moss) into the Devon. The next in order is Broich, which rises at Maddy-Moss, and, after a run northwards of about three miles, joins the Devon at Back Hill House. Grodwell (a fine branch of Broich) rises on the back of Ben Cleugh, and joins the larger stream about a mile north from Maddy-Moss. We come next to Frandy Burn, and then Glensherup, both fine fishing streams. It is on the latter the reservoir for Dunfermline waterworks has been constructed. The next tributary is Glenquhey Burn, with its fine branch the Garthland. This, I believe, is the most severely fished stream of any in the Ochils, being within a convenient distance of Dollar, with its large population of boys. After passing Dollar, we then come to Tillicoultry Burn, with its two branches—Daiglen and Gannel Burns—which would have plenty of trout but for being so constantly fished. Some good trout are occasionally got in the linns in the glen. The next in order are Alva and Menstrie Burns, neither of which I have fished, but which, I have no doubt, would, like the others, have plenty of trout if they could only get a little rest. There are an immense number of smaller streams all the way round, but none of which are big enough to tempt the angler, although I have no doubt many of them contain trout.

On the north side of the Ochils, the stream corresponding to the Devon on the south side is the Allan. It has many tributaries from the Ochils—the Wharry, Millstone, Buttergask, Ogilvie, and Danny Burns, the last joining it at Blackford. The Ruthven and the Water of May are tributaries of the Earn. The highest hill on the north side of the Ochil range is Craigrossie, to the south-east of Auchterarder.

The north and south Queichs drain the south side of the eastern portion of the Ochils, and fall into Lochleven ; while the Farg, which rises north from Milnathort, falls into the Earn, about three miles from where it joins the Tay. The great north road runs through Glenfarg—one of the most picturesque glens in Scotland. The greater portion of it is beautifully wooded ; while the road, which follows close to the stream in all its serpentine windings through the really beautiful, and, at places, narrow glen, presents at every turn fresh glimpses of magnificent scenery, and forms quite an enchanting drive. Before the railway from Edinburgh to Perth was formed, the stage and mail coaches between those two cities ran through Glenfarg, and many is the time I have passed through it, seated on the top of the ' Defiance.'

In the Statistical Account of Scotland, the Rev. Mr. Osborne says, in connection with the hill burns of Tillicoultry : ' No trout were ever discovered in the Glooming-side Burn (the name then given to Gannel Burn), though it has plenty of water, and remarkably fine streams and pools. Trouts have even been put into

W. Banks & Son Edin.

DEVILS MILL, RUMBLING BRIDGE.

it, but without the desired effect. This is supposed to arise from some bed of sulphur, or other mineral hurtful to fish, over which the burn passes.'

This belief had got so impressed on the minds of the community, that no one ever thought of fishing in this burn, until, forty years after Mr. Osborne wrote this Account, this popular fallacy was discovered by the merest accident. The late Mr. John Ure, and his brother-in-law Mr. James Archibald (then a boy of 14), started one morning, in the year 1833, for a day's fishing on the hills, and, the morning being very misty, they got a little confused as to where they were. Mr. Ure intended fishing down Greenhorn, and Mr. Archibald down Grodwell and Broich, and they were to meet on Devon. Under Mr. Ure's directions, his young brother-in-law got to what he considered was Grodwell, and hadn't fished long till some excellent trout were caught; and when he reached what he considered was Broich, he soon got a basket of large, beautiful trout. After getting well down the burn, he came, to his surprise, to some impassable rocks, that he never remembered having seen on Broich before, and was quite puzzled as to where he was. On getting above the rocks, and pursuing his way a little, what was his astonishment to find, that in place of landing at Back Hill House, as he expected, the town of Tillicoultry was lying down below him. The truth then flashed upon him that he had been fishing all day in Glooming-side Burn (Gannel), which was popularly believed, for at least forty years, to have had no trout in it; and here was his basket filled with large, beautiful trout. When Mr. Ure came home, he could scarcely credit what had taken place, till he himself, on a subsequent occasion, had verified the truth of it. And now the secret *was out*, but was for a considerable time made known only to a very few. One of those fortunate few, however, came home invariably with such a well-filled basket, that it quite excited the curiosity and envy of one of his acquaintances, and he determined that he would watch him some day when he knew he was going for a day's fishing, and learn the secret. Accordingly, he started up to the hills one morning before him, and concealed himself at a convenient spot where he could watch his movements. What then was his profound surprise when he discovered that he went down to Gannel Burn. This discovery, as may be supposed, took the whole village by surprise, and a sorrowful time of it the poor trout had after that, as a perfect rush of fishers at once took place to the doomed burn, and the '*big ones*' quickly disappeared.

TILLICOULTRY A MANUFACTURING VILLAGE IN THE DAYS OF QUEEN MARY.

We learn from Mr. Watson's interesting book, that as far back as the days of Queen Mary (in the middle of the sixteenth century) cloth was manufactured in Tillicoultry, which afterwards became so famous that it established for itself a name throughout the country, and when other places commenced to make the same kind of cloth, it had to be sold by the name of the place where it was first introduced : it was called ' Tillicoultry serge,' and no other name would take the market ;—in the same way as, at the present day, thousands of spindles of stocking-yarn are sold annually as ' Alloa yarn ' that never saw Alloa.

When alluding to the now celebrated Alloa stocking-yarn, I may, in passing, refer to the very small beginning of the business at Kilncraigs, which has turned out to

be one of the largest (if not *the* largest) of the kind in
the kingdom. When old Mr. Paton commenced business, he had only two carding engines; and now the
firm of John Paton, Son, & Co., are possessed of forty-
nine sets of machines (147 carding engines) at their three
works at Kilncraigs, Keillersbrae, and Clackmannan.

Mr. Watson tells us that the writer of the old
Statistical Account of Scotland describes the serge 'as
being a species of shaloon, having worsted warp and
yarn waft.' The weavers were called ' websters ' in
those days, and are mentioned in the oldest records of
the kirk-session of Tillicoultry.

With reference to the introduction of this serge
into Tillicoultry, Mr. Watson says : 'What led to its
being located here can only be conjectured. David I.
received into his dominions a number of Flemish
refugees, driven in 1155 from England by Henry II.,
whose policy thus contrasted unfavourably with that of
Henry I., who had gladly given encouragement to the
honest Flemish artisans to settle in his realms. It is
not improbable that the woollen manufacture was introduced into this part of Scotland by some of these
Flemish refugees. Amongst the natural advantages in
its favour may be reckoned the supply of wool which
was obtained from the pastoral lands of the Ochils.
When this supply was insufficient, it was not uncommon for the guidwife to go to Edinburgh for a
stone of wool, which she carried home on her shoulders,
and afterwards spun into yarn in the intervals of her
household duties.'

'The cloth was sold at an average price of 1s. per
yard. . . . It is much to be regretted,' says the Rev.
Mr. Osborne (who was minister of Tillicoultry from
1774 till 1795), ' that more attention is not paid to

the manufacture in the place where it was invented, or
at least brought to the greatest perfection. About fifty
years ago, a serge web from Alva would not sell in the
market while one from Tillicoultry remained unsold.
But this is by no means the case at present. The
author of this Account can give no precise statement
of the quantity of serge wrought here, as the stamp-
master keeps no list. He supposes, however, that he
stamps annually 7000 ells of serge, and an equal
quantity of plaiding. Some of the weavers are now
employed in making muslins; but as this branch is
still in its infancy, it is impossible to say with what
advantage it may be attended.'

It couldn't have been because of the water-power
that Tillicoultry got established so early as a place of
manufacture, for no power of any kind was used in
those days. It must have been, as Mr. Watson suggests, because of the abundant supply of wool close at
hand. Wool was then carded with little hand cards,
and the yarn spun by women in their own homes, and
neither the carding-engine nor the spinning-mule had
then been heard of.

The mode then in use for milling the blankets and
plaidings made from these home-spun yarns was by
the women tramping them with their feet, which must
have been a very slow, tiresome, and unsatisfactory
process; and the very first object aimed at by our
early manufacturers was to get a more efficient method
introduced for accomplishing this object. This, therefore,
more than for carding and spinning, was the purpose
for which the first mills here were principally erected,
and to which the water-power was first applied.
Waulk mills were erected, which would not only do
the work much more efficiently and quicker than

before, but would also relieve the guidwives of what must have been a very laborious and fatiguing operation (although tradition says they were rather jealous of the innovation).

FIRST MILLS ERECTED IN TILLICOULTRY.

As far as can be learned, the first waulk mill erected on Tillicoultry Burn was put up in the open air, by one Thomas Harrower, in the end of last century; but where this mill stood no one seems now to know. About this time, also, the first spinning mill in Tillicoultry was built, by three brothers, named John, Duncan, and William Christie, which is still standing, although used now only as a place of storage, and the attic as a hand-loom weaving shop. It is situated above the upper bridge, and is known as the Old Mill of Castle Mills.

The Messrs. Christie being very pushing men, particularly the brother John, they soon found the one little mill too small for their operations; and they then built what is known as the Old Mill of Robert Archibald & Sons' works, at the 'middle of the town,' which was the second mill built in the village. In both places waulk mills were erected, and a great trade carried on in milling goods to the country people round about.

The first carding-engine in Tillicoultry was erected in 'Betty Burns' house' (a little two-storied building opposite the boiler-house door of Mr. Walker's mill), and must have been of a very primitive kind; but whether it belonged to the Messrs. Christie or some other one, there seems to be some doubt. It was driven by the hand, and must have been quite as

laborious an operation as the tread-mill, but of course
a decided step in advance of the little old hand cards.
As to the correctness, however, of this being the mode
of driving the first carder ever started here, there can
be no doubt, as the old man who had been employed at
it told my informant (Mr. David Paton) that this was
the way it was driven.

The water-wheel for Messrs. Christie's first mill was
close to the east wall of the building, on the outside,
and was removed only about a dozen of years ago,
power not being then required for this part of the
works.

About the same time that this primitive mode of
driving a carding-engine was in operation in Tillicoultry, there was one started in Alva, driven by a
horse, and Mr. Edward Moir recollects well of seeing it
in operation. A company of eight or nine gentlemen
were connected with it, and they afterwards built the
next mill above Castle Mills in Tillicoultry, and it
often went by the name of the Horse Mill (in consequence of the company's peculiar start in Alva),
although no horse was ever used in it. It was more
generally called the Company Mill, by which name it
is still known. Six members of this company were
named—James Balfour, James Ritchie, James Morrison,
David Drysdale, William Rennie, John Cairns, and
the name of the firm was James Balfour & Co. A
waulk mill was at once erected by them here, and
each member of the company got his turn at milling ;
and a worthy old lady of our village remembers well
of the goods being regularly carried along from Alva,
on their backs, to get milled here ; and so great were
the demands on this mill, and so much difficulty
experienced in getting their goods milled in time, that

it was often like to lead to misunderstandings and unpleasantness amongst the various members of the company.

Mr. John Christie built and lived in Burnside House, Tillicoultry, the residence at present of Mr. Scott and family, and for such a long period of years previously of Mr. Robert Archibald and family. He was the most active of the three brothers ; and when he died, the other two gave up the business, and emigrated to America. As far as I have been able to learn, this would be about the year 1814 or 1815, as the old 'middle of the town mill' stood silent for two or three years previous to Mr. Robert Archibald acquiring it.

INVENTION OF THE SPINNING-MULE.

About the year 1764 a very great discovery was made (from a very trifling circumstance) in the art of spinning, which completely revolutionized this branch of industry, and led to results the importance and magnitude of which it is impossible to estimate. A spinning-wheel having been accidentally overturned, the spindle (although in a vertical position) continued to revolve, and the yarn to spin, as before,—the thread slipping over the point of the spindle at every revolution ; and the idea at once suggested itself to James Hargreaves, that if one spindle could do so, why not a number ? and here was 'the germ' of the spinning-mule. A small machine was at once constructed, with eight spindles only, and got christened by the name of the Spinning Jenny. In 1770 Arkwright invented a spinning frame, which was a great improvement upon the first attempt of Hargreaves ; but the real author of the spinning-mule was Samuel Crompton, who, by combining the invention of Hargreaves with that of Arkwright, gave us that invaluable machine which has continued in use ever since. This combination, or mongrel sort of machine, had suggested the name of ' mule ' for it, and hence it was so named. The vastness of the results gained by its adoption may be judged of from the fact that, in place of one spindle (as in the old spinning-wheel), revolving at a very slow speed, a pair of mules have frequently 1000 spindles, revolving about 4000 times a minute! Samuel Crompton was born at Bolton in 1753, and died in 1827.

Several attempts were made, first by William Kelly, of Lanark Mills, Scotland, Mr. Smith of Deanston, and others, to make the spinning-mule self-acting ; but the real inventor of the self-acting mule was Richard Roberts, born in North Wales in 1789. It was not till 1830—when he also invented the quadrant motion —that the success of the self-actor may be dated.

The head stock of the self-actor is a most ingenious piece of mechanism, and shows Mr. Roberts to have been a man of rare genius. Had a worthy man who lived in Dollar when the wool mill was first started there, and who, on first seeing through it, was much impressed with the ingeniousness of some of the then primitive machinery, lived to see the self-acting mule, he would have had more reason for the exclamation of surprise he gave utterance to, and which so much amused his hearers : ' The works of nature are very wonderful, but the works of man are more wonderful still.' Mr. Smith of Deanston was the first to introduce the self-actors into Scotland, and to adapt them for *wool* spinning; and the first self-acting mules for this purpose *in the United Kingdom* were fitted up by him for Mr. William Drysdale, Braehead, Alva, and Messrs. Robert Archibald & Sons, Tillicoultry. Great improvements, however, have been made on them since then, and they are now as near perfection as it is possible almost for them to be.

A very primitive sort of spinning machine, called a Jack, was what was generally in use in Tillicoultry in the beginning of this century; and it, like the carding-engine, was driven by the hand. Afterwards the spinning frame was introduced, driven at first also by the hand. An uncle of Mr. Edward Moir's (a Mr. David Lawson), wrought one of those hand-spinning frames in the attic of Christie's first mill.

The hand-billey and hand-mules were the next improvements introduced, and they were driven partly by hand and partly by power. When the self-acting head stock was perfected, it was applied to both the billey and the mules, and self-acting machines of both kinds were gradually introduced; and now, unless in small country mills, hand-mules or billeys are rarely to be seen.

Some very extensive machine works are now in existence for the production of carding and spinning machinery, one work alone, in England, giving employment to between 5000 and 6000 hands.

INVENTION OF THE PIECING MACHINE AND CONDENSER.

When carding wool by the carding-engine was first introduced (and for long afterwards), the rovings, or rolls of wool that were taken off the carder (from sheets

of card set apart from each other) for the foundation
of the thread, were rubbed together or 'pieced' at the
billey *by the hand;* which must have caused very
irregular yarn, and no little pain to the children's hands,
which were often bleeding at night. By and by, however, a piecing machine was invented by Mr. John
Archibald of Keillersbrae ('Uncle John,' so called to
distinguish him from his nephew of the same name), for
joining these rovings together, which did the work much
more efficiently, and dispensed with the services of some
three or four children for each billey. This piecing
machine was afterwards greatly improved, first by James
Melrose & Sons, Hawick, and was afterwards further
improved by Mr. Archibald of Devondale ; and where
billeys are still used, Mr. Archibald's is the one now in
general favour.

The mechanical genius of our age being ever at work,
an invention was afterwards brought out that dispensed
entirely with piecing machines and billeys, and which
not only saves time and labour, but makes a much
better yarn,—that was the condenser. In place of the
wool coming off the carder in thick rolls, from sheets of
card placed across the machine, it comes off the
condenser doffer (from narrow rings of card put round
it) in small, continuous slivers, and thus no piecing is
required ; and these are rubbed or 'condensed' into
small soft threads, which are then taken to the mules
and spun into yarn. This mode of making yarn is now
almost universally adopted, although piecing machines
and billeys are still in use in small country mills, and
even hand-piecing, I learned the other day, is not yet
quite extinct. As the billey is a large machine, and
takes up a great deal of room, a great saving of space
has been effected by its discontinuance.

DETAILED NOTICE OF THE PUBLIC WORKS IN TILLICOULTRY.

About the beginning of the present century, three brothers, named John, William, and Robert Archibald, left Tullibody and started a small woollen mill in Menstrie. They were destined afterwards to play an important part in the opening up of the woollen trade at the foot of the Ochils, and some of their descendants are at the present day proprietors of some of our largest manufacturing establishments. Either direct or by marriage, the descendants of those three brothers are, or have been, connected with nine of our public works, viz. the original mill at Menstrie ; Strude Mill, Alva ; Craigfoot Mill ; Robert Archibald & Sons ; J. & D. Paton's, and J. & R. Archibald's works, Devondale, Tillicoultry ; Keillersbrae, Gaberston, and Kilncraigs Works, Alloa. Mr. William Archibald, of Strude Mill, Alva, and Mr. John Archibald, of Keillersbrae (' Uncle John '), were sons of Mr. John Archibald, of Menstrie. Messrs. John, William, and Andrew Archibald, of Keillersbrae new mill, were grandsons ; Mrs. Lambert, of Gaberston, was a grand-daughter ; and Mrs. John Thomson Paton, of Norwood, a great-grand-daughter. The first Mrs. James Paton and first Mrs. David Paton were daughters of Mr. William Archibald, of Craigfoot, Tillicoultry, one of the three brothers who left Tullibody for Menstrie.

In 1806 Mr. William Archibald left Menstrie for Tillicoultry, and built the third mill of the village at Craigfoot (which at present forms the back wing of the works), and pushed the trade very successfully for a great many years.

Mr. Robert followed him in 1817 (two or three

years after the Messrs. Christie left Tillicoultry), and bought the second mill they built at 'the middle of the town,' and started the firm of Robert Archibald & Sons.

Mr. John continued in Menstrie, and carried on the original mill there, which was after his death carried on for such a very long period by his two sons, Mr. Andrew and Mr. Peter.

The village of Tullibody (we learn from the Statistical Account) claims a comparatively high antiquity. About the year 834, Kenneth king of the Scots assembled his army on the rising ground close to where this village now stands, previous to attacking the army of the Picts, under Druskein, their monarch, who had put Kenneth's father to death, and on whom he was determined to be revenged. Having completely defeated the Pictish army, he pursued them to the river Forth, near Stirling, and thus fully accomplished the object he had in view. Returning to where his army had encamped before the battle, he caused a stone to be erected where the royal standard had stood, as a memorial of the victory; and this stone was only removed about fifty years ago. The spot, however, where it stood is well known to the neighbourhood, and still receives the name of the ' stan'in' stane.' 'A little to the east of the field where the main body of his army was encamped, he also founded a village, which he called "Tirlybothy" (since varied into Tullibodie and Tullibody), a name originally signifying "the oath of the croft." Such was the origin of this village. For upwards of three centuries subsequent to the period mentioned, little of its history is known.' Tullibody Church is a small but venerable edifice, having been built by David I., king of Scotland, in the year 1149, nearly 700 years ago. Two years previous to this, he had also built the

splendid Abbey of Cambuskenneth, on the very spot
where his royal ancestor Kenneth gave the fatal blow
to the Pictish dominion. 'The churches, with their
tithes and pertinents, belonging to this abbey, were those
of Clackmannan with its chapels, Tillicoultry, Kincardine, St. Ninians with its chapels, Alva, Tullibody,
with its chapels at Alloa, etc. The first Abbot was
called Alfredius.'

For upwards of 400 years the rites of the Roman
Catholic faith were celebrated in Tullibody Church. It
is recorded that in the year 1559 it was unroofed by
the French, who under Monsieur d'Oysel were retreat-
ing on Stirling, on hearing that the English fleet had
arrived on the coast of Fife. Kirkcaldy of Grange, in
order to arrest their progress, broke down the bridge of
Tullibody over the Devon, about a mile to the west of
the village, and the French unroofed the church, and
used the materials for a temporary bridge. The church
continued in this dismantled state for about 200 years,
when it was roofed in by George Abercromby, Esq., of
Tullibody, and used by the family as a place of sepulture.
About fifty years ago it was fitted up by subscription as
a preaching station.

In order to get water to such a high situation as
Craigfoot (fixed on by Mr. William Archibald for his
mill), two formidable undertakings had to be accomplished,—the formation of a dam far up the glen, and
the construction of a lade to convey the water from
it to the mill. From the great length of the latter, and
the immense depth of it at one part below the surface
(20 feet at least), they must have cost him, or the laird,
a very large sum of money.

Besides other machinery, Mr. Archibald put in a
waulk mill at Craigfoot, which soon brought him into

trouble with the inhabitants of the village. There being no common sewer in those days, as at present, the waulk mill water was run into the burn above the village; and the inhabitants naturally rebelled against this, and insisted on its being stopped. Not being able to come to a satisfactory arrangement about it, the guidwives of the village, armed with axes, hammers, etc., proceeded in a body to the dam-head, and soon completely demolished it, which of course would put a stop to all operations at the mill, and throw all the workers idle. It was, however, got quietly constructed a second time during the night, soon after; and no sooner was this known than the irate ladies proceeded to the work of destruction again, and soon made short work of the erection. (Mr. Moir, who informed me of these incidents, remembers well of the excitement caused in the village at the time, and of seeing the wives proceeding with their implements to the work of destruction.) Things having now reached a crisis, something required to be done to put a stop to such a state of matters, and Mr. Johnstone of Alva (the present Mr. Johnstone's father) allowed Mr. Archibald to make a sewer for the dirty water down through his plantation into the sunk fence of his fields; and thus an end was put to the strife.

About the same time that Mr. Robert Archibald got the middle of the town mill, the other mill built by the Messrs. Christie at Castle Mills was bought by a Mr. Robert Walker, who came about that time, with a grown-up family, from Galashiels.

In 1820 his two eldest sons, James and George, built the mill immediately below the upper bridge, and started business there under the firm of J. & G. Walker. This business was very successfully carried on for a great many years, and when Mr. George Walker (the present Mr. Robert Walker's father) died, he was possessed of very considerable wealth.

Shortly after this mill was built, a younger brother, named Andrew, built the New Mill of Castle Mills; and when I came to Tillicoultry, it went always by the name of 'Andrew Walker's Mill.' He erected a large gaswork within the grounds, which supplied (in addition to his own works) the whole of the village with gas. A very singular coincidence in connection with this family was, that those three brothers, and also another brother, all died at the age of forty-two. James died in 1832, George in 1841, and Andrew in 1843.

The next mill to Craigfoot was built by a Mr. James Dawson, about the year 1811 or 1812. Although now the property of Mr. Cairns, it still goes by the name of Dawson's Mill. The one below it was built about the same time by the company of gentlemen from Alva (James Balfour & Co.) already referred to, and is still known by its old name of 'The Company Mill;' but at one time, as already stated, it was occasionally called 'The Horse Mill.'

After Mr. William Archibald's death in 1826, his business was carried on for thirteen years by Mrs. Archibald; and hence Craigfoot was very generally called, when I came to Tillicoultry, 'The Widow's Mill.' One of Mr. Archibald's first carding-engines still stands in the Old Mill (unused),—a relic of bygone days.

In 1838 the large new mill (with its giant water wheel—35 feet diameter) was built; and in 1839 Mr. Archibald's two sons, Mr. John and Mr. Robert, took over the business, and started the new firm of J. & R. Archibald, which has been carried on so successfully now for forty-three years. The business extended so rapidly, that in 1846 the first part of the extensive works at Devonvale was built, which has since been added to so very largely. Mr. John died on the 1st of January 1848, at the early age of thirty-five; and the business has, since then, been carried on solely by Mr. Robert, until his sons were old enough to assist him in it. Craigfoot and Devonvale were both carried on by the firm till 1851, when the business was transferred entirely to Devonvale. The class of goods manufactured by this firm is of the very best description, and has long taken a first place in the tweed trade,—the name of ' *Devonvale* ' (as with the Alloa yarn) being a sufficient guarantee for the superiority of the goods. As a specimen of some of our modern manufacturing premises, I herewith give a view of their extensive and beautiful works. The mill to the south (the last one built) is generally considered ' *a model* ' of what a spinning mill ought to be. Those works are situated very near the railway station. Mr. William Archibald's old rent-book for the water-power and feu-duty of Craigfoot Mill, which commenced in 1807, is in my possession now, and is still used by me when paying these to James Johnstone, Esq. of Alva. This little passbook is very interesting, from the fact that it is now seventy-five years old, and is quite a little history in itself regarding the factors on the Alva estate. A Mr. Alexander Littlejohn received the first feu-duty for Craigfoot Mill in 1807, and he continued factor till 1816. Mr. John M'Laren, of Burnside of Alva, followed him, and continued for the long period of thirty-one years. Mr. James Kerr, writer in Stirling, succeeded Mr. M'Laren, and acted for nine years; and then Mr. James Moir, banker, Alloa, followed, and continued for fifteen years, from 1859 till 1874; and after his death Mr. Archibald

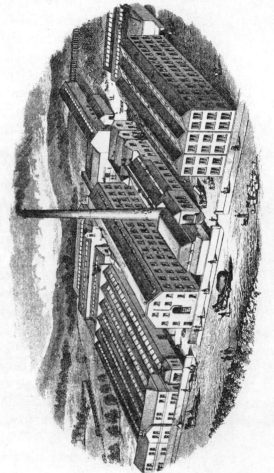

DEVONVALE WORKS,

Moir, his brother, was appointed, and is now factor at the present time.

The most extensive and prosperous business in our village was commenced in 1824, by Messrs. James and David Paton (the two eldest sons of the late Mr. John Paton of Kilncraigs, Alloa), under the firm of J. & D. Paton. From a very small beginning, this business gradually extended, and has been for many years the principal mainstay of the working population of Tillicoultry, a very large number of hands being employed by the firm. Their goods have long been celebrated throughout the country; and at the first Great Exhibition in London in 1851, they obtained the gold medal for their exhibits. The works now cover a very large piece of ground, and contain seventeen sets of carding and spinning machinery, and upwards of 250 power and hand looms. Both gentlemen have given very largely of their wealth for the cause of Christ, both at home and abroad; and Mr. James built a very handsome manse for the U.P. Church here, bought the old manse, and presented it to the village for a British Workman Public House.

Mr. James's two sons—Mr. John and Mr. James—were taken into the firm a great many years ago, and up till 1875 both together took the active management of the business. In that year, however, on the 3rd of March, Mr. James was taken away at the early age of forty-three; and his death was a great blow to all the friends, and must have been particularly so to his brother, with whom he had all along been associated. Since that year the management has devolved principally upon Mr. John; and the loss of the counsel and assistance of such a shrewd, active business young man as Mr. James was, must have been very much felt by him. Mr. James left £5000 to found an orphanage in his native village; and this has proved a very great blessing indeed. A beautiful house was erected in Ochil Road, and, under the motherly care of Mrs. Currie, who was appointed to take charge of it, from eight to ten orphans have been enjoying all the comforts of a nice home, and having not only their temporal but their eternal interests well looked after.

From the present state of the health of Mr. James Paton, senior, and the long-existing copartnery being about to expire, it is more than probable that Mr. John will after this be the sole proprietor of these extensive works and prosperous business.

The firm of Robert Archibald & Sons consisted of the father and four sons,—Messrs. William, Robert, Duncan, and James. The original mill, bought by the firm in 1817, proving too small for their increasing business, their new mill was built in 1836, adjoining which there have since been added a very large power-loom shed and other extensive premises, and further extensions are in contemplation. For many years they have been doing a large and profitable business, and have become quite celebrated throughout the trade as the makers of the finest woollen shirtings that are produced; and they are, in consequence, kept always busy, and give employment to a very large number of hands. They have now close on one hundred power-looms, besides a large number of hand-looms, and manufacture tweeds as well as shirtings. Mr. Archibald, senior, died in 1849. Mr. William retired from the business in 1858. Mr. Robert died in 1868, and Mr. Duncan in 1874. The only member of the original firm then left being Mr. James, he assumed as partners, in 1875, Mr. Robert, his son, and Mr. Alexander Scott.

Mr. Archibald has laid our village under a deep debt of gratitude to him, by building a very handsome tower to our Town Hall, and providing it with a clock and bell, at a cost of about £1500. He has been, for upwards of a dozen years, the much-respected captain of our rifle volunteer corps, and is proprietor of the beautiful villa of Beechwood.

When referring to our Town Hall, or 'Popular Institute,' as it is generally called, I think it right to state, in passing, that the inhabitants of Tillicoultry are indebted to the late Mr. Archibald Browning, junior, for initiating the movement which culminated in the erection of this fine building. It was he who gave it the name it still bears; and both he and his brother, the late Mr. Richard Browning, exerted themselves most energetically in getting funds raised for carrying the project through. It has been a great acquisition to our town, and I think it ought not to be forgotten who the originator of it was, and to whose exertions the village is so largely indebted for the carrying out of the scheme to a successful termination. Mr. Archibald Browning, junior, died on August 2nd, 1854. Mr. Richard died on the 25th July 1855; and Miss Catherine Browning in March 1855.

FIRST POST-OFFICE IN TILLICOULTRY.

Mr. Thomas Walker was appointed the first postmaster in Tillicoultry in 1833, and his widow is still our much-respected post-mistress; so that Mrs. Walker has now been connected with our post-office for the long period of fifty years. Mr. Walker died in 1852. I am sure I only express the feeling of the whole community when I say, that during all those years our post-office has been conducted to the entire satisfaction of every one.

During the long period that Mrs. Walker has been at the head of our post-office here, she has seen many improvements introduced in connection with it,—such as the penny postage, the savings bank, money orders, the telegraph, etc., and she informs the writer that they frequently send and receive more telegrams in a day now, than they used to do of letters in the days of the dear postage. The active duties of the office are now being conducted by her son, Mr. William, her daughter, Miss Walker, and her grand-daughter, Miss Anderson.

The telegraph from Alloa to Tillicoultry was constructed in the year 1860, and cost above £100, one half of which was paid by the railway company, and the other half by the inhabitants of Tillicoultry. And so little faith had the telegraph company in its being self-supporting, that a few individuals had to guarantee the clerk's salary for the first year, before they would agree to erect it. The guarantors, however, were never called upon to make up any deficiency, as it was largely taken advantage of from the very first, and proved quite a paying concern.

In the year 1839, a Mr. John Henderson built the only woollen mill at that time not in connection with the burn, the water for the steam-engine of which was got from the Ladies' Well. This mill was three stories in height, and was occupied by three different parties, viz. Mr. Henderson, Mr. Thomson Dawson, and Mr. Alexander Robertson. It was destined, however, to have a very short career; for, one evening about seven o'clock, in the spring of 1842, the cry of 'Fire!' was suddenly heard, and in little more than an hour the whole pile was reduced to ashes, and nothing left but the blackened walls. I don't know how the others stood for insurance, but Mr. Robertson was not insured at all, and this disastrous fire completely ruined him. From being a manufacturer on a considerable scale, he was at once reduced to a weaver, and was working on the loom when I came to Tillicoultry. This Alexander Robertson (or 'Sandy Robertson,' as he was generally called) was, by the way, one of our very best curlers,— although left-handed,—and considered one of the best skips in the club. The walls of this mill stood for thirty-five years in a ruinous state, and it was always known as 'The Burnt Mill.' In 1874, however, it was turned again into a substantial building, by having its walls thoroughly repaired and roofed in ; and now a large portion of it is turned into a dye-house, and carried on by Mr. George Brownlee—on a very exten- sive scale—as the Lady-Well Dyeworks, where 'plant' of the very newest description has been introduced, in- cluding a large blue vat; while the other portion of it has been turned into a weaving shop, and carried on by Messrs. Robert Archibald & Sons. In place, then, of this part of the village having a desolate and forlorn look, as it had for such a long period, all is now bustle and activity.

It may not be out of place here, when taking notice of 'The Burnt Mill,' to give our own experience of fires (those ever-to-be-dreaded calamities of the mill- owner), of which we have, unfortunately, had more than the average share.

In the month of March 1858, when busy in the office one day, we were suddenly startled by seeing a black cloud of smoke rushing past the office window, and, on running out to see what was the cause of it,

were horrified to find the big mill on fire, and the
under flat filled with smoke as black as coal. We at
once gave the mill up for lost, and were, of course, in
a great state of excitement and alarm. However, not
a moment had to be lost, and a double row of hands
was at once arranged from the mill door to the lade,
and a constant supply of water poured on the floor
above where the fire was, which was effectual in drown-
ing it out before the fire-engines (which had been sent
for) arrived. This was not accomplished, however, till
upwards of £300 of damage had been done. Nothing,
however, could have saved the mill but for an extraordinary feat that was performed by our old ex-foreman,
John Gentles. The day having been a very dull one,
the gas was partially lighted through the mill, and the
sagacious old man saw at a glance that unless the big
meter could be turned off, the mill was sure to be lost.
But here was the difficulty. The entrance door of the
flat where the fire was was, at the one end of the mill,
and the meter stood at the other end, and to reach it
the whole length of the mill had to be traversed
through black, suffocating smoke, in which I couldn't
have lived for a second or two ; and into this pit this
devoted man plunged, walked the whole length of the
mill, turned off the meter, walked all the way back
again, and came out alive. How this feat was accomplished astonished every one, as it really seemed little
short of a miracle.

After the fire was extinguished, we found that
this noble act of his had saved the mill. The main
gas-pipe had been blazing, and was melted fully half-
way along the mill, and in another minute or two it
would have reached the perpendicular ' main ' for the
flats above ; and then all would have been lost.

This fire originated at the teazer, while teazing a batch of Angola wool, which is a very inflammable material when once it is started ; and but for the abundant supply of water immediately at hand, all efforts to put it out would have proved abortive.

After this fire, the teazer was at once removed to a separate house, and a stopcock placed on the gas supply pipe, outside the mill.

Our next experience of this dreaded foe was in the month of July 1863. On arriving at the railway station from the east one day, a messenger was waiting for me with the unwelcome news that the teazer-house, with all its contents, was burned down. This of course was very vexatious, as it seriously interfered with our operations, and, until new teazers could be got ready, would put us very much about. However, with the kind help of our neighbours, we had just to do the best we could, and use every precaution possible against a like calamity occurring again.

Our next and last experience of fire (and I earnestly hope it may be the last) was a much more serious affair than the teazer-house, and, happening as it did through the night, gave us all a dreadful shock. About three o'clock on a dark, foggy morning in November 1876, I was awakened out of a sound sleep by hearing ' Fire ! fire ! fire !' shouted most lustily in front of our house ; and on opening the window and asking where it was, was answered, 'At the head i' toon' (a very common designation for our works). On looking in the direction of the mill, I was alarmed to see the whole heavens lighted up with a very big fire, and concluded at once it was all over with the big mill. I found, however, on getting to the street—and to my great relief — that it was only the dry-house. This building, however (125 feet long, and two stories and attics high), was ablaze from end to end, and a very formidable-looking fire it was. The fire-engines were at work when I got there, but all they could do was to prevent the fire spreading to the other buildings, and in this they were successful; but the dry-house, with all its contents, was burned to the ground. In rebuilding this house, we made it ' fire-proof' by putting in an iron floor above the flue. An old saying is, ' Burnt bairns dread the fire,' and our repeated experiences of this ' useful servant but bad master' has made us use every possible precaution against the recurrence of a like calamity. An *extincteur* and six pails of water are kept always ready in every flat of the mill, and all material that is apt to take fire spontaneously removed from the mill daily.

The millwright and machine works of Messrs. James Wardlaw & Sons have been in existence since 1824, and were established at first by a Mr. Robert Hall, Mr. William Ross, and Mr. James Wardlaw (Sir Henry Wardlaw, Baronet's, father), under the firm of Robert Hall & Co., and have all along been the only public works of the kind in the village. Their first premises were situated nearly opposite the Crown Hotel, and were the first buildings on the south side of the High Street. Their present works were erected in 1839, and after the death of Mr. Ross and Mr. Hall (the former about forty years ago, and the latter some fifteen years afterwards), the firm was changed to James Wardlaw & Sons. Sir Henry Wardlaw, Bart., is now the sole partner of this old-established firm. He succeeded to the baronetcy in 1877, on the death of his father's cousin, Sir Archibald Wardlaw, Bart., who lived in Edinburgh. The Wardlaw baronetcy dates from

1631; and for a very full and interesting account of it from that time till the present day, see the *Tillicoultry News* of January the 18th, 1882, or Dod's *Peerage, Baronetage, and Knighthood of Great Britain and Ireland* for 1882. Mr. James Wardlaw (Sir Henry's father) died in 1867.

In this record of the early public works of Tillicoultry, I must not omit to mention a fine mill that was erected by a Mr. Robert Marshall, about the year 1836. Not having been successful in business, this mill came into the market for sale, and was bought by the Messrs. Paton, and is now incorporated with their works. It is the end building of the south wing, and on the right-hand side as you enter their works.

CHAPTER IX.

COMMENCEMENT OF THE VILLAGE OF DEVONSIDE.

HAVING taken notice of all the old works established in Tillicoultry, I will now go over to Devonside, that thriving little suburb of our village, most of which is built on the property of James Blair, Esq., of Glenfoot.

The first mill erected there was built by Mr. Thomas Monteith, of Tillicoultry, in 1834; and in company with his son William, the business was carried on there for a great many years under the firm of Thomas Monteith & Son. The erection of this mill was the commencement of the village of Devonside. It is the second one from the bridge.

The ground being once broken there, others soon followed Mr. Monteith's example, and in 1836 the mill next the bridge was built by a company of three,— Messrs. James Henderson, David Moir, and Robert Walker (a cousin of the present Mr. Robert Walker).

In the same year, also, the mill to the west of Messrs. Monteith's was built by the following gentlemen,—Messrs. David Anderson, Robert Blackwood, Peter Miller, William Young, and William Smith, senior; and the one to the west of it again, in 1841, by Messrs. James and John Hunter, Robert Young, and William Smith, junior.

Beyond this last spinning mill, and farthest west of the public works, a weaving factory was erected by

Messrs. James and Matthew Thomson about the year 1845 or 1846.

The first little one-storied mill at Keillersbrae was built by a Mr. Keiller; and hence the name of the works. Mr. William Archibald (son of Mr. John Archibald of Menstrie) who was for some little time at the commencement of his business career in company with old Mr. Paton at Kilncraigs, Alloa, left there, and bought Keillersbrae Mill, and commenced business there by himself. He added two stories to the mill, thus greatly increasing it in size. His brother, Mr. John Archibald ('Uncle John'), was carrying on spinning at this time in Strude Mill, Alva, and Mr. William's two sons, John and William, were there with him. Mr. William, senior, and Uncle John then changed places,—Mr. William going up to Strude Mill, and his brother coming down to Keillersbrae. Mr. William spun stocking-yarn at Keillersbrae, and continued to do so at Strude Mill, Alva; while Uncle John started the business of machine-maker at Keillersbrae, and continued this as long as he lived.

After a time, Mr. William Archibald, senior, built Keillersbrae new mill, for his three sons, John, William, and Andrew, and an extensive manufacturing business was carried on by them there for a number of years. To celebrate the start of it, a grand ball was held in one of the flats of the mill, at which there was a very large attendance,—the largest, I believe, that was ever seen in the county. The walls were all hung with tartan, and great preparations made for it, and the entertainment passed off with great spirit, and proved a great success.

When this business was given up, Mr. Andrew joined his father at Strude Mill, Alva, where a most

N

prosperous business of stocking-yarn spinning had been established by him, and the firm was then changed to William Archibald, Son, & Co. This business is still being most successfully carried on—under the same old firm—by their successors, Messrs. Cowan and Dawson.

GARTMORN DAM.

When referring to Keillersbrae, it may not be uninteresting to learn how the water-power for this mill and other mills in Alloa was got. From the last Statistical Account of the parish of Alloa (drawn up by the late Mr. William Brodie, teacher, Alloa, in 1840), we learn that about the year 1700 (183 years ago), 'the celebrated John, Earl of Mar, who had a great mechanical turn, and attended much to the improvement of hydraulic machinery (the steam-engine not having then been brought forward), caused a strong dam-head to be thrown across the Black Devon at Forrest Mill, in the parish of Clackmannan, by which he raised the bed of this river 16 feet higher. From the top of this dam-head he carried an aqueduct westward about four miles, which carried the water into Gartmorn Dam, perhaps the largest artificial lake in Scotland, covering, when full, above 160 imperial acres. It is about 160 feet above the level of the Forth, and 92 feet above Alloa. In some places it is 36 or 37 feet deep, being sufficient to carry a seventy-four gun ship. Prior to 1785, only a temporary dyke existed. A dam-head was then built of hewn stone, measuring upwards of 320 yards, at an expense of several thousand pounds. In the year 1827 this embankment threatened to give way, in which case it would have swept away, with the torrent of its waters, all the lower part of the town of Alloa lying in its course. It then underwent a complete repair by Mr. John Craich, the present manager of the colliery, at an expense of only £300; whereas, in the opinion of a celebrated engineer, the sum necessary for performing the work effectually would be £3500. This lake is situated at the north-east extremity of the parish, about two miles from Alloa. Its waters form a permanent supply for driving the hydraulic machinery of the Alloa Colliery and the water-wheels of various manufactories.'

The Earl of Mar could find no person in Scotland of sufficient skill to carry out this undertaking, and in order that he might have the most eminent person then known, he brought Mr. Sorocold, a mining engineer, from Wales, at a great expense, to carry the scheme through. The primary object the Earl had in view in the formation of Gartmorn was to get a supply of water for the water-engine at the coal-pit near Carsebridge.

The hamlet of Forrest Mill, from the neighbourhood of which the supply of water is got for Gartmorn, was in the year 1766 the abode of Michael Bruce, the poet of Lochleven, where he taught a little school. He was suffering from consumption when he went there, and on his journey thither from Kinnesswood his horse stumbled with him when passing through the Black Devon, and, all dripping and wet, he arrived at his lodgings there. This greatly accelerated his malady, which so soon after terminated fatally. In writing to his friend Mr. David Pearson, he says: 'The next letter you receive from me, *if ever you receive another*, will be dated 1767. . . . I lead a melancholy kind of life in this place. . . . I have some evening scholars, the attending on whom, though few, so fatigues me that the rest of the night I am quite dull and low-spirited. Yet I have some lucid intervals, in the time of which I can study pretty well.'

Michael Bruce was the author of some of the finest compositions in the English language,— such as the 'Ode to the Cuckoo,' 'Lochleven,' 'The Last Day,' etc.; while some of the most beautiful of our para-phrases were written by him. Dr. M'Kelvie of Bal-geddie, in his biography of him, clearly proves that Logan pilfered a great many of Bruce's finest poems, and published them as his own. He died in 1767, at the early age of twenty-one, and was buried in Port-moak churchyard. His father, Alexander Bruce, was a weaver in Kinnesswood. He died in 1772.

SUBSEQUENT OCCUPIERS OF SOME OF THE MILLS.
GREAT FLOOD OF 1877.

I will now refer shortly to those who occupied some of the mills after the original proprietors of them had passed away, and to some public works of more recent date.

On Mr. James Dawson and his family emigrating to America, Messrs. J. & D. Paton and J. & R. Archibald jointly leased the south part of this mill, having each one set of machines in it; while J. & R. Archibald occupied the northern portion of it by themselves as a weaving shop. In 1848 both of them gave up the whole mill in my favour, and it was here I commenced manufacturing in that year, and continued in it by myself till 1851. The south part, as before, was filled with carding and spinning machinery; my office, ware-room, etc., were in the first flat of the north mill;

while the upper flat, attics, and back weaving shop were filled with looms.

In 1851 Mr. Archibald of Devonvale and I entered into partnership under the firm of William Gibson & Co., and the office was removed to Craigfoot; but we still retained Dawson's Mill, and have continued the tenants of it ever since. Mr. William Anderson was my first warper, and continued in my employment for a number of years. He then commenced manufacturing on his own account in the old U.P. church (latterly Mr. Browning's), and carried on a very successful business there till his death, which took place in 1870, when forty-two years of age.

The next mill below Dawson's (The Horse, or Company Mill) was long carried on by Mr. Alexander Harrower of Alva; and on his death a Mr. Scott became the tenant of it, and continued in it for many years. Edward Meiklejohn & Co. next became the tenants, and are carrying it on at the present time.

On the death of Mr. Andrew Walker, his widow carried on Castle Mills for a considerable time, under the management of Mr. Robert Fotheringham. After his death they were bought by Alexander M'Nab, Esq., of Glenochil, in 1849; and the firm of William Hutcheson & Co. was then started, and carried on the works till the disastrous flood of 1877, under the management of Mr. William Hutcheson, and for a short time after that under that of his son, Mr. Abraham Hutcheson.

This great flood having had such an important bearing on the present position of these works, I will now briefly refer to it. On the 28th of August 1877, one of the most calamitous floods took place along the front of the Ochil range that was ever known in the memory of man, and that will be long remembered in Dollar and

Tillicoultry, where it seemed to have wrought the greatest havoc. After a deluging rain had continued for some time, the clouds seemed to have suddenly opened out in a series of waterspouts all over the front part of the Ochils, and, without a moment's warning, Tillicoultry Burn came raging down in one mighty wall of water of some seven or eight feet high, carrying everything before it, and causing great destruction to property all down through the village, leaving a scene behind it that would be almost impossible to describe.

First in its progress of destruction, a large portion of Mr. Hutcheson's power-loom shed, with the ground between it and the burn, and the strong-built wall at the side of the burn, with the private bridge inside the works, were all swept away without a moment's warning. Then the upper public bridge was left almost a total wreck, the water careering over the high parapet wall on the north side of it, forming one of the most frightful scenes ever beheld. On passing this bridge the raging rush of waters then scooped out a large portion of Upper Mill Street, right across to the houses, and to the depth of some seven or eight feet, the pavement for a good distance being carried away, and the houses escaping total destruction only by a hairbreadth. On leaving this point the mighty torrent then proceeded to the work of destruction on both sides of the burn. The street on the west side was, for a long distance and to a great depth, carried wholly away, and the east end of Mr. Ure's house was completely wrecked, leaving the rooms inside quite exposed. On the east side of the burn it knocked down the wall at the back of Mr. Browning's property, and, rushing through the east portion of it, filled the rooms to a great depth,—Mrs. Alexander's invalid son John narrowly escaping being drowned, and was carried out with considerable difficulty. After sweeping away the Tea Bridge, and committing terrible havoc on both sides of the burn, part of the water then rushed along Frederick Street (the 'Howdub') and down Stirling Street (to the great consternation of the inhabitants), a deep stream of water the whole width of the street, having never been seen there before since ever it was a street.

On the main body of the water reaching the lower bridge, it then swept along the High Street in a great volume of some three feet deep; and so frightened were the inhabitants, that some of them were leaping out at their back windows into the gardens behind, and great damage was done to both dwelling-houses and shops.

But the most painful part of the whole catastrophe was the lamentable loss of life connected with it, my good kind friend and neighbour Mr. Hutcheson and one of his workwomen (Isabella Miller, daughter of Mr. Crystal Miller, Union Street) being swept away with it and drowned. Mr. Hutcheson and his dyer, William Stillie, were in conversation at the end of the private bridge within the works; and Isabella Miller was, at the critical moment, passing them, when, without the slightest warning, the ground gave way under their feet, and bridge and all three were engulfed and swept away with the torrent. The dyer got hold of the iron stanchions in the windows of Mr. Walker's house below the public bridge, and held on there till assistance came to him; but the other two were carried away and drowned, Mr. Hutcheson's body being got down at the Oak Mill, and Isabella Miller's a good way down the Devon. This lamentable loss of life cast quite a gloom over the town, and great sympathy was felt for the bereaved families.

It would be next to impossible to give a proper idea of the spectacle our burnside presented after the flood had passed, and it would have required to have been seen to be properly realized. The channel of the burn was not only filled to the brim with immense boulders, but was actually piled above this in many places to a great height ; while the streets on both sides of the burn were covered with débris to a great depth, some huge blocks of stone, of above a ton weight, being carried right across the streets and deposited on the pavement.

The channel of the burn being thus so completely filled up, the water had to make new channels for itself on both sides of its usual course, the one below the upper bridge being of great depth and extent, and entirely stopping all traffic for a considerable time. The pavement in many places was torn up and damaged to a serious extent; and, besides the great loss to private individuals, it took about £2000 to repair the damage to our streets and burn. The dam-head up in the glen was filled to the brim (it is 35 feet deep) with débris, and cost the manufacturers above £100 to get it cleared out and repaired. (*The Alloa Illustrated Family Almanac* of 1878 gives some very good views of the destruction caused by this extraordinary flood, both in Tillicoultry and Dollar,—those two places having suffered more than any of the other villages along the foot of the Ochils,—and they are repeated again in that of 1879.)

The effects of those waterspouts can be seen all over the south side of the Ochil range, great holes having been made at many places, and the earth from these to the bottom of the glens torn up to a great depth, showing clearly that these great floods in Dollar and Tillicoultry were caused by a series of waterspouts. A fine specimen of this can be seen in the front of Ellieston Hill above Harviestoun West Lodge, where a deep and wide scaur was made from the top of the hill to the foot, and a large portion of a field covered to a great depth with the débris. The lodge was surrounded with water, and the wall opposite it, on the south side of the turnpike road, was tumbled over into the field. In rebuilding this wall, Mr. Orr made several loopholes through it at its base, in case of a similar catastrophe again happening. It is to be hoped, however, they will never be required.

In the Statistical Account of Tillicoultry parish, Mr. Osborne gives an account of a very heavy flood on the Devon, but doesn't refer to Tillicoultry Burn at all. From the great destruction caused by the Devon, however, it is more than probable that its tributaries— Tillicoultry and Dollar Burns, etc.—would also commit great havoc. He says :—

'A very remarkable and uncommon flood happened in September 1785, which carried away a prodigious quantity of corn, broke down a stone bridge at the Rack Mill in Dollar, and occasioned other very extraordinary damage. The river rose in four or five hours more than 13 feet above its usual height at Tillicoultry bridge. A woman who was assisting a farmer in removing his corn, on the south side, was forced away by the rapidity and violence of the stream, and brought in safety to the opposite bank. Her clothes had made her float on the surface of the water, though she was carried down about a quarter of a mile.'

Shortly after Mr. Hutcheson's death, the works were brought into the market for sale, and, lying adjacent to our other premises at Craigfoot, we bought them, and have carried them on ever since.

Having, for business purposes, got views taken of both our works, I herewith insert them; and they will give a better idea than any description can give of what some of the first mills in Tillicoultry are like. The mill in the foreground of the view of Craigfoot Mill is Dawson's Mill, which we only lease; while the large mill at the foot of the Craig is the one built by J. & R. Archibald in 1838; and the wing behind it (increased in height when the big mill was built) by Mr. William Archibald, their father, in 1806.

The one-storied building below the entrance gate (in the view of Castle Mill) is the upper end of the first mill in Tillicoultry, built by the Messrs. Christie in the end of last century. The large mill is the one built by Mr. Andrew Walker; while the dwelling-house is on the site of the old castle formerly referred to, and from which the works got their name. The roof of a house in the foreground of this view (on the opposite side of the street from the entrance gate) is the roof of the Horse, or Company Mill.

After the deaths of Messrs. James and George Walker, their mill (immediately below the upper bridge) was carried on for a considerable time by Mrs. George Walker, under the management of Mr. Thomson Dawson, until Mr. Robert Walker, her son, was the length of managing it himself. This mill, the Bridge Mill at Devonside, and Thomas Monteith & Son's mill (subsequently acquired by him), are now Mr. Walker's property.

In 1860 the finishing works of Mr. Robert Drysdale were erected, and have been carried on with great spirit ever since. The grounds around these works are laid out with great taste, and are quite an ornament to this entrance to the village.

CRAIGFOOT MILL

CASTLE MILL

From a very old document that has been put into my
hands, I find Mr. Drysdale can trace his genealogy back
to the beginning of the sixteenth century. I herewith
give a copy of it in full:—

'On the twentieth day of May, one thousand five
hundred and three years,—

'We, Thomas, William, and James Douglas, sons of the
departed Thomas Douglas, of Brushwood-Haugh, in the
parish of Drysdale and shire of Dumfries, left our native
place for the reason here assigned, viz.: Defending our
just and lawful rights against our unjust neighbour,
Johnstone of Greenstone-hill, who being determined to
bring water to his mill through our property, and having
obtained leave of his friend the king, began his operations
on Monday the 16th May. We prevented him by force.

'The next day he brought twenty of his vassals to carry
on the work. We, with two friends and three servants
(eight in all), attacked Johnstone with his twenty; and in
the contest fourteen of his men were killed, along with
their base leader.

'A report of these proceedings was carried to the king,
and we were obliged to fly (the tocsin being sounded).
We took shelter under the shadow of the Ochil Hills in a
lonely valley on the river Devon.

'After having lived there two full years, we returned
home in disguise, but found all our property in the
possession of Johnstone's friends, and a great reward
offered for our lives. We having purchased a small shot
called the Haugh of Dollar, and changed our names to
the name of our native parish, and are clearly in mind to
spend the residue of our days under the ope of the Ochils,
and wish the name of Drysdale to flourish in the lonely
valley. The king passed through this with his court on
the 12th of June 1506, going from Stirling to Falkland;
dined on Halliday's green (an eastern neighbour), but we
were not known.'

The foregoing document had been preserved among

the descendants of those three brothers Douglas (now known by the name of Drysdale), and copied first by Symon Drysdale, of the Haugh of Dollar, in the year 1620 ; by Robert Drysdale, of Tillicoultry, in 1708, and renewed at different times since then.

The spinning mill of Edward Senior & Co. was erected in 1864, and the Oak Mill—built by a limited liability company—in 1873. The latter is now the property of Mr. Gill, and was acquired by him in 1881.

MANUFACTURING FIRMS WHO DIDN'T SPIN YARNS.

I will now shortly take notice of a number of manufacturing firms who did not spin, but bought all their yarns, and some of whom carried on pretty extensive businesses ; and foremost amongst these is the enterprising firm of Monteith & Drysdale. The original partners of this firm were Mr. James Monteith and Mr. Alexander Drysdale ; and they commenced business in 1836, in premises nearly opposite J. & G. Walker's Mill, and carried on, also, the dye-house in connection with this mill for a good many years. They had no spinning mill at this time, but bought all their yarns. Mr. James Monteith died in 1847, and the business for a long period was carried on solely by Mr. Drysdale, until his son, Mr. James, was of age to assist him in it. In 1849, Mr. Drysdale bought the two mills at Devonside, to the west of Thomas Monteith & Son's, and built the fine new spinning mill there, with the large power-loom shed and other premises that now form their extensive works. Mr. Drysdale retired from the business in 1871, and it is now being carried on by Mr. James Drysdale and Mr. Allan Ritchie, under the same old firm of Monteith & Drysdale.

The next business I will refer to is that of our respected townsman, Mr. Robert Young. Mr. Young, as already noticed, was one of the original partners of the firm who built the farthest west spinning mill at Devonside in 1841 ; so that he has now been for the long period of forty-one years one of our local manufacturers. In 1860 he built those commodious premises in the Moss Road, where he has carried on his business ever since. He is now assisted in it—and has been for a good many years —by his son Mr. James.

The firm of James Dick & Co. commenced business in part of the Bridge Mill at Devonside in 1850. The original partners of this firm were—Messrs. James Dick, Thomas Graham, William Miller, and Andrew Lane. Mr. Dick retired from the firm about two years after it was started, but the name of the firm continued the same as before. Mr. Miller died a few years after Mr. Dick left the business ; and it was afterwards carried on by the two remaining partners, Mr. Graham and Mr. Lane. Their premises were changed, first from the Bridge Mill to part of Thomas Monteith & Son's Mill, and ultimately to the weaving factory at the west end of Devonside (erected by the Messrs. Thomson), where they continued in business for nearly twenty years. The business was given up in 1877, Mr. Graham still residing amongst us in retirement, and Mr. Lane removing to Glasgow.

MANUFACTURERS AT ONE TIME IN BUSINESS IN TILLICOULTRY.

It may not be uninteresting to give a list of some of the firms that were at one time in the trade here, most of the members of which have either passed away or have left the district :—

William M'Ewan.
Charles Fleming.
James M'Ilwraith.
John Crichton.
James Galloway, sen.
Charles Dickson.
Alexander Robertson.
Thomson Dawson.
John Davidson.
John Wardlaw.
John Monteith.
John Dow.
Andrew Miller (left Tillicoultry in 1840).
James Wallace.
James Alexander.
James Anderson.

William Anderson.
Robert Drysdale.
Robert Graham.
John Tulloch.
James Rolland.
Andrew Scotland. ⎫
John Kirk.　　　 ⎬ In company.
William Young.　 ⎭
James Robertson. ⎫
William Miller.　 ⎬ In company.
James Chalmers.　 ⎭
Thomas Syme & Co.
Alexander Hunter.
Alexander Stewart.
R. & J. Monteith.
Inverarity & Co.

Firms carrying on manufacturing here at present, but who don't spin yarns, as follows :—

Hendry Brothers, Tillicoultry.
Thomas Marshall,　　　,,
Robert Young,　　　　,,
Drysdale, Hunter, & Co., ,,
Archibald Leishman,　　,,

John Meiklejohn, Tillicoultry.
Mr. Lawson,　　　　　,,
Andrew Miller,　　　　,,
Alexander Nicol, Devonside.
William Brown & Co., ,,

GOODS MANUFACTURED AT THE FOOT OF THE OCHILS.

John Archibald & Sons, of Menstrie, commenced at a very early period to manufacture broadcloth, but did not continue long at this branch of business. They were for a long time, however, quite celebrated for a superior class of tartan trouserings, which were at one time very fashionable, and greatly worn. They were the first, I believe, to introduce power - looms into the district, having had some at work as far back as fifty years ago. J. & R. Archibald, also, from the very commencement of their business, occasionally made broadcloths and trouserings; but they formed a very small portion of their business.

Up till the year 1830, the principal goods, however, manufactured at the foot of the Ochils were blankets and plaidings, which were generally taken to Perth market, and exposed on stalls for sale; and this continued, less or more, up till the year 1840. About the year 1830, a new manufacture was introduced to the locality, which gradually superseded the weightier and plainer goods, and eventually became the staple trade of the district,—that was, the manufacture of tartans. These goods by and by became so fashionable, that no lady considered herself dressed without a tartan plaid or shawl; and tartan dresses became very fashionable also. The result was, that the demand for them became so great, the trade soon assumed gigantic proportions, and the villages of Alva and Tillicoultry increased rapidly in size and population. New firms started by the dozen; and in the town of Alva alone there could not have been fewer at one time than from thirty to forty manufacturing firms.

About the year 1854 a change of fashion took place, which had a serious effect on the tartan trade, and which eventually drove some of our largest firms out of it altogether; and that was, the introduction of cloaks or jackets as an article of dress, which have continued ever since, in one shape or another, to hold their place in the favour of the ladies. It was then that J. & R. Archibald, Devonvale, J. & D. Paton, Robert Archibald & Sons, and ourselves, commenced to make tweeds or shirtings, which ultimately resulted in J. & R. Archibald giving up the manufacture of tartans entirely, and confining themselves almost wholly to tweeds; Robert Archibald & Sons, to shirtings and tweeds; J. & D.

Paton, to tweeds, shirtings, shawls, and other new fabrics introduced from time to time; while for ourselves we gave up manufacturing altogether, and have since 1858 carried on the spinning trade alone. Tartan handkerchiefs, however, are still largely manufactured, and give employment to a great many hands; but the yarn for them is principally spun in Belgium, and at prices the Scotch spinner cannot compete with; and hence the spinning trade of this district is not much benefited by this class of work. Raised shawls are now also (and have been for a number of years) manufactured largely, and have at present every appearance of continuing to be for some time a staple part of our local trade.

Some very extensive businesses are being carried on in Alva at the present time, in various branches of our local manufactures; but it would take too long time, and is out of the scope of these jottings, to refer to them in detail. I may just mention, however, the large and prosperous business of Messrs. William Ross & Sons, whose extensive and beautiful premises add greatly to the business look of the town of Alva. The late Mr. William Ross, sen., was a man of great taste, and had a thorough practical knowledge of his business, and did much to raise the fame of our local manufactures, from the beauty of the goods he produced. He was the architect of his own fortune, and was much esteemed and respected by all who had the pleasure of his acquaintance. The business is now being carried on with great energy by four of his sons, and gives employment to a very large number of hands. Mr. Ross commenced business in 1838, and, from a small beginning, gradually enlarged his premises as his business increased on his hands. In 1865 he erected the fine spinning mill and other premises at Brookfield, which are at present being about doubled in size. He died on the 12th of July 1877, aged sixty-eight years, leaving his widow and six of a family to mourn his loss.

I will only refer to one of the old firms that at one time existed in Alva, and which occupied a very prominent place in the tartan shawl trade, and carried on a very extensive business for a great many years,—the Messrs. Drysdale of Boll Mill. There were three brothers of them,—William, John, and Robert. In addition to their spinning mill and other premises, they erected in 1845 that fine weaving shop which is such a conspicuous building in the higher part of Alva, and gives such a business-like look to the town. The two youngest brothers were cut off while quite young men,— the youngest one, Mr. Robert, first (he died in 1852), and Mr. John in 1854, and Mr. William alone now survives. Their premises are now occupied by Messrs. Tod & Duncan, Ramage & Sutherland, and others.

While Alva and Tillicoultry were from time to time adding to the number of their mills and factories, and increasing in size and population yearly, Menstrie stood almost stationary for a great many years, having only the original woollen mill built by the three brothers Archibald in the beginning of this century. In the year 1864, however, the first part of the very extensive and beautiful works of Messrs. Drummond & Johnston was erected, which has since been added to so very largely; and now their works give employment to a great number of hands, and must have proved of immense benefit to the village. The original mill of the brothers Archibald is still being carried on; but it has now passed into the hands of Messrs. Robert Archibald & Sons, Tillicoultry, the head of which firm was one of the three brothers.

O

A woollen mill has been carried on for a very long period at Glendevon. Previous to 1850, Mr. Thomas Elliot was the tenant of it; but in that year Mr. John Clayton succeeded him, and greatly enlarged and improved the premises. Since Mr. Clayton's death, the works have been carried on by his sons, under the firm of Clayton Brothers. They are situated at the foot of Glenquhey Burn, and near to its junction with the Devon.

When referring to Glendevon reminds me of an amusing incident in connection with a worthy farmer, who lived in the glen about forty years ago, and who, when a young man, had studied for the ministry, and preached for some little time. He and two of his companions had been in a very jovial, happy mood one day, and when walking along the road, were 'chaffing' the passers-by, or, as we would say in Scotland, 'taking their fun off them;' when, meeting a decent-looking old man, one of them addressed him thus,—' Well, my man, and who art thou?' To which he at once most suitably replied,—' I am the servant of Saul the son of Kish, sent to seek his father's asses, and lo and behold! I have found three of them.' The three students had met their match in the decent old body, and must have felt rather 'taken down a peg' when they got this reply; and, I hope, were more prudent in future.

This story of the minister farmer of Glendevon brings to mind a rather good story in connection with farms. A herd laddie was quarrelled by his mistress for running into the house whenever it came on a slight shower of rain, and was told he was not to do so unless it was an *even-down pour*. One day, shortly after this, it was a regular drenching day from morning till night, and to the guidwife's astonishment there was no word of the laddie coming in; but at last, at night, he made his appearance, thoroughly soaked through and through; and when taken to task for his strange conduct, he said he was told not to come in unless it was an *even*-down pour; 'now it wasna that, for it was *squint*.' This worthy lady would see the necessity of being more particular as to the terms she used to this 'young hopeful' after this.

The principal warehouses in Glasgow, in the early days of the tartan trade, that confined themselves exclusively to this branch of business were—Robert M'Kay & Co., Drysdales & Wilson, John Wilson, Sons, & Co., Charles M'Donald & Co., and Gow, Butler, & Co.; while some of the general warehouses, such as J. & W. Campbell & Co., William M'Laren, Sons, & Co., John M'Intyre & Co., Stewart & M'Donald, Tannahill & Robertson, Broadfoot, Brand, Thomson, & Co., etc., did a very large trade in them. The Messrs. Drysdale (of Drysdales & Wilson)—William, Archibald Browning, and Thomas Monteith—were natives of Tillicoultry, and had always a very 'warm side' to their native village. Their father, Mr. Alexander Drysdale, was an elder for a very long period in the United Presbyterian Church here, and lived in Stirling Street, in the house at present owned and occupied by Mr. James Hay. Mr. Thomas is the only brother that now survives.

Mr. Robert M'Kay visited the hill foots himself for many years, and bought all the goods required by his firm; and Mr. Gibb (brother of Mr. Gibb in Dollar) then succeeded him, and for a very long period was the shawl buyer for this firm.

Mr. James Liddell was buyer for a considerable time for Broadfoot, Brand, Thomson, & Co.; and latterly for John Wilson, Sons, & Co. He was then succeeded by Mr. George Wilson, one of the sons of the firm.

Mr. David Pye was one of the first shawl buyers for J. & W. Campbell & Co., and Mr. Robb succeeded him, and continued their buyer for a great many years.

Mr. Butler himself for a long period bought all the goods required by Gow, Butler, & Co., and was a frequent visitor at the foot of the Ochils. He was then succeeded by Mr. Fisher, who after Mr. Butler's death joined the firm, which was then· changed to Gow, Fisher, & Co. Mr. Smith was shawl buyer for Stewart & M'Donald for a good many years. Mr. Charles M'Donald was a regular visitor at the hill foots for a long period ; and Mr. Alexander Paterson was afterwards made buyer for Mr. M'Donald's firm.

In order to stimulate the demand for tartan dress goods, a ball took place in Alva about the year 1845 or 1846, at which all the ladies had to be dressed in tartan, which was very largely attended, and proved a great success. This assembly was very much talked about for many a day after, and was always spoken of as the 'tartan ball.' Tartan dresses came to be very fashionable and generally worn, and dress goods was a most prosperous branch of the tartan manufacture at the foot of the Ochils for many years. *All-wool* tartans, however, were too expensive for 'the million ; ' and this gave rise to a new branch of the trade, which soon assumed enormous proportions. This was the manufacture of Gala tartans, which were made with *cotton* warps and *woollen* wefts, and came in at a much more moderate price than *all-wool* goods, and the quantity of them manufactured for many years was something fabulous. This branch of the trade, however, didn't benefit the 'hill foots' at all, as these goods were made principally in Auchterarder, Perth, and Glasgow.

CHAPTER X.

IN the beginning of this century a Mr. Burns was parish teacher in Tillicoultry, and the school and school-house were then in the centre of Braehead Street, at present occupied by Mr. John Jack. Mr. Burns left Tillicoultry, and was succeeded by Mr. Kirk (father of Mr. Thomas Kirk, late classical teacher in Dollar Academy) in the year 1810. When Mr. William Christie (one of the three brothers) emigrated to America, about the year 1814, the heritors bought his house, situated at the east end of the upper bridge, for the parish teacher's dwelling-house, and the little house at the east end of it for the school, and thither Mr. Kirk was removed.

For a considerable length of time Mr. Kirk went up to Harviestoun Castle, and gave Mr. Craufurd Tait's family private lessons, and had the distinguished honour of teaching the Archbishop of Canterbury his 'A B C.'

Mr. Kirk was much esteemed in Tillicoultry, but the village was soon deprived of his services, as he was cut off at the early age of thirty-four. A memorial stone was erected to him in the old churchyard, with the following inscription :—

Sacred
to the memory of
MR. JOHN KIRK,
late schoolmaster of the
parish of Tillicoultry,
who died the 6th day of
September 1821,
aged 34 years.

Much lamented.

Mrs. Kirk was left a widow at the early age of twenty-eight, and lived to the long age of eighty years.

On the death of Mr. Kirk, Mr. Watt succeeded him, and he was parish teacher when I came to Tillicoultry in 1847. Mr. Watt was an eccentric man from the very first, but latterly became so much so, that his school dwindled away so seriously, that the heritors were compelled to take some steps for the better educating of the youth of the village; and as Mr. Watt couldn't be turned away, they built the fine school and schoolhouse at present occupied by Mr. Watson, and as the infant school, and called it a 'subscription school,' and appointed Mr. W. W. Clugstone teacher. After the opening of this school, Mr. Watt's gradually melted away till he had only one scholar left, and it was said to be very amusing to hear him dismiss this school *of one boy:* ' Now, go all out in order, and make no noise.'

Mr. Watt delighted in what we Scotch folks call ' lang-nebbit words; ' and one day he asked his class (a number were then in it) ' what a mountain was ? ' when a little urchin at once promptly replied, ' A big hill, sir.' ' No, no,' Mr. Watt answered, ' I wouldn't say that ; it is an excrescence or protuberance on the face of the globe.'

As he lived alone in the big schoolhouse, with no

one to take care of him, the interior of the house presented a most lamentable appearance; while the schoolhouse was utterly wrecked by the boys. It was a nightly spectacle to see a dozen of boys round him, tormenting the poor man, who latterly was really a fitter subject for an asylum than being nominally the parish teacher.

On Mr. Watt's death, Mr. M'Turk was appointed parish teacher, and the new school and schoolhouse, where Mr. Watson at present lives, were then called what they really were from the beginning, ' *The parish school and schoolhouse.*' Mr. Clugstone, not having been successful in getting the appointment, started an adventure school for himself, which he continued for some years, but eventually gave it up, and opened a druggist's shop, which he carried on till his death. He was also collector of poor rates for a considerable time.

The Rev. Archibald Browning was settled in Tillicoultry in the year 1818, and almost from the first he managed to combine with his pastoral duties the education of a few boarder-pupils, with whom were associated such day-scholars as the district afforded. The school gradually increased till it demanded his whole attention, and accordingly in 1825 he resigned his ministerial charge. His seminary became quite famous throughout the country, and he had frequently close on forty boarders. He was an excellent teacher, and pupils came from neighbouring villages to attend his classes. The late Rev. Dr. Eadie of Glasgow was one of his scholars, travelling all the way from Alva to be under him. He was afterwards one of his assistant teachers for about three years.

In the *Life of Dr. Eadie* by Dr. James Brown, the late Rev. George Gilfillan of Dundee furnished the author with 'Reminiscences of Dr. Eadie,' in which Mr. Browning's name is so prominently and favourably referred to, that I think it will not be out of place here to give a few extracts from them. Mr. Gilfillan says : 'At college I knew Dr. Eadie somewhat, though slightly. . . . I remember him in the Logic class in the year 1828, a fair-haired youth of eighteen. . . . My more intimate connection with Dr. Eadie began somewhat later, and resulted from our common acquaintance with a very remarkable man, to whom I owe much, and Dr. Eadie owed a vast deal more,—the late Rev. Archibald Browning of Tillicoultry. I have since that time met with and listened to the conversational eloquence of some of the most eminent men of our age, such as De Quincey, Professor Wilson, Leigh Hunt, and Thomas Carlyle, but I never was more impressed by any of these than I was the first evening I spent in Mr. Browning's company. His talk was in a very high degree racy, original, suggestive, and stimulating,—full of humour and anecdote, as well as of bold speculation, and glimpses of far-stretching thought. I know not whether young men were more attracted by his fearless speculations, by his frank manners, by his public preaching, or by his private converse. He shone in various departments, being an admirable teacher of the young, a powerful though peculiar preacher, and a very popular lecturer on social and political questions, such as Temperance and the People's Charter. . . . Some of his pupils and assistant teachers, such as the Rev. David Connal of Bo'ness, and the Rev. William Smith of Bannockburn, to whom they ultimately stood in the relation of sons-in-law, and whom, even while widely severed in political and religious views, they regarded to the last with reverence and love. But Dr. Eadie's debt to him might be

called, in Milton's language, 'a debt immense,' and in-
volved a duty of ' endless gratitude,' which we have no
doubt was duly paid.

' Mr. Browning taught him first at his day school,
assisted him to go to college, received him (after an
estrangement which lasted for more than a year, and which
was produced, as Eadie often acknowledged, entirely by
his own fault) back into favour again, installed him as
tutor in his academy, and assisted him in going to the
Divinity Hall of the United Secession Church to prosecute
his studies for the ministry. . . . It was while John Eadie
was an assistant teacher in Mr. Browning's academy that I
first really met him. Mr. Browning, while visiting my
late lamented brother in Stirling, where I then was, had
kindly invited me to spend a few days in his house at
Tillicoultry. Here I found Eadie very busy and happy
in his tutorial work. I remember spending a long May
holiday with him and some of the pupils of the academy
among the Ochil Hills, and our chief employment was
reading Shakespeare. . . . Eadie had been a good
classical scholar at college, and had profited much afterwards in Latin and Greek while assisting Mr. Browning.'

Having lived for many years in Cairnton House (Mr.
Browning's property, and adjoining his own dwelling-
house), I ever found him a kind and obliging neighbour,
and our intercourse together as landlord and tenant
was always of the pleasantest kind. We had a joint
garden, and thus came very much in contact with each
other. As Mr. Gilfillan says, he was indeed ' a very
remarkable man,' and occupied a very prominent position in Tillicoultry for the long period of forty years.

Although he lived to a good old age, the heavy
bereavements he experienced in the death of the three
of his family previously noticed (all grown up), a few

years before his own death, would no doubt hasten that event, which took place very suddenly in the end.

Mr. Browning was born in Strathaven in 1785, and died in the year 1858, aged seventy-three years.

Miss Browning (afterwards Mrs. George Paton) carried on a very successful school for some time, being latterly assisted in it by her husband.

Mr. Peter Dow had a school for a great many years at the head of Union Street; Mr. John Stalker had one in Ochil Street; Miss Cameron, and then Mr. Roxburgh, had one in Frederick Street; and Miss Ramage (afterwards Mrs. Dr. Brodie) conducted an infant school for a good many years in the schoolroom of Messrs. J. & D. Paton's works.

When Mr. David Paton built the schoolrooms and schoolhouse in Stirling Street, one of the best teachers Tillicoultry ever possessed was appointed,—the late Mr. M'Gregor, from Tullibody, who proved himself a most efficient and excellent teacher, and who was very much esteemed by every one.

After this the Education Act came into operation, and our present public school was built, and Mr. Watson appointed head master, than whom we could not have got a better man for the situation. This school has prospered greatly under his management and the able staff of teachers that have from time to time been appointed under him; and the attendance is at present very large, and the school in the highest state of efficiency.

I will now just name the bankers who have been in Tillicoultry. Mr. John Sawers was appointed the first agent of the Edinburgh and Leith Bank (afterwards the Edinburgh and Glasgow, and ultimately the Clydesdale), and Mr. John Thomson succeeded him, and was followed by Mr. A. P. Lorrimer, and then Mr. William Gray. The Union Bank had, for long after I came to Tillicoultry, no branch here, but Mr. Brydie of Alloa sent up some of his representatives twice a week, and transacted business in Cargill's Hotel; and in this capacity the present much-respected head inspector of the Union Bank—Mr. A. B. Henderson—visited us regularly for a considerable time. When the Union Bank opened a branch here, Mr. John Kirk of Tullibody was appointed agent, and continued so till his death, and during all the long years he was in Tillicoultry was very much esteemed by every one. He was succeeded by Mr. William Hunter, our present agent.

When the Royal Bank opened a branch here, Mr. A. P. Lorrimer was appointed the first agent, and at his death Mr. Alexander Wilson was appointed. When the Royal Bank resolved to discontinue their branch here, the Clydesdale bought the fine building the Royal had built, and transferred their office from the building at the foot of Stirling Street (where it had been so long) to it, and appointed Mr. Jasper Robertson, the present agent, to succeed Mr. Gray.

In the old Statistical Account of Tillicoultry parish, the Rev. Andrew Rynd's admission to the kirk of Tillicoultry is put down as 1648.

The following is a complete list of those who followed him, with the years of their ordination.

Rev. John Forrest, 1669.
 ,, Robert Keith, 1676.
 ,, Robert Gourlay, 1692.
 ,, John Taylor, 1714.
 ,, Robert Duncan, 1728.
 ,, Alexander Steedman, 1731.

Rev. James Gourlay, 1765.
 ,, William Osborne, 1774.
 ,, Alex. Stirling, LL.D. 1795.
 ,, Henry Anderson, 1808.
 ,, David Smith, 1843.

When the Rev. Archibald Browning retired from the U.P. Church, the Rev. James Young succeeded him, and preached for some time in the old Church in Mill Street. The present U.P. Church in High Street was opened on the 4th October 1840, Mr. Young being minister. Mr. Edward Moir precented on the occasion. The Rev. George Hunter was ordained as Mr. Young's successor, on the 20th of August 1844. He died on the 2nd of March 1871, aged sixty-one years. The Rev. William Galletly succeeded Mr. Hunter, and is minister at the present time.

When the new U.P. Church was opened, Mr. Browning formed a congregation of his own (not in connection with any body) in the old church, and preached there till within a week of his death, although he had been in failing health for a good many years previously.

The Rev. Henry Anderson left the Established Church at the Disruption in 1843, and was the first minister in the Free Church here. He was born on the 9th of February 1779, and died on the 12th of August 1845, aged sixty-six years. The Rev. David Smith succeeded him in the Established Church at the Disruption. On the death of Mr. Smith last year, the Rev. Joseph Conn was appointed his successor.

We have in the village, besides the churches already named, the Evangelical Union Church, the Congregational Church, and the Hall of the Christian Brethren.

The Rev. Henry Anderson lived only two years after the Disruption, and was succeeded by the Rev. David Black, who continued minister of the Free Church for a long number of years. The Rev. James Brown succeeded Mr. Black; and when he was translated to St. Peter's Church, Glasgow, the Rev. William Miller—the present minister—was appointed his successor.

The Evangelical Union Chapel was opened in August 1853, but the congregation was formed two years before that, and met in Messrs. Paton's schoolroom. Their first minister was the Rev. John Anderson, who remained with them for two years. His successors up till the present time have been—the Rev. John Andrew, Rev. James Strachan, Rev. Alexander Nairn, and the Rev. James Davidson, who is their minister now.

The Congregational Church was built in the year 1876, but the congregation was formed three years before this, and worshipped in the Popular Institute Hall. Their first minister was the Rev. E. D. Solomon, who was inducted in August 1873 ; and when he was translated to Glasgow, he was succeeded by their present minister, the Rev. Arthur Smith.

The Hall of the Christian Brethren, in Hamilton Street, was built by Mr. Archibald of Devonvale in the year 1864.

DEPARTED TOWNSMEN.

I may here give the names of a few of our townsmen who have passed away since I came to Tillicoultry, and whose deaths have not been otherwise referred to in this book:—Mr. John Cargill, of the Crown Hotel; Mr. John Donaldson, a well-known merchant in Union Street; Mr. Thomas M'Guffie; Mr. William Monteith, and his son Mr. Robert, clothiers in High Street; Mr. Thomas Monteith, clothier, High Street ; Mr. John Ure, merchant in Mill Street ; Mr. John Monteith, manufacturer ; old Laird Ritchie, and Mr. James, his son; Mr. Dewar, factor ; Mr. Cairns, farmer, and his two sons, Mr. Robert and Mr. John ; Mr. M'Turk, teacher; Mr. Graham

Paterson, wright, and his whole family of four sons and one daughter,—Mrs. Paterson being left alone to mourn their deaths ; Mr. Thomson Dawson ; old Mr. Abraham Hutchison ; Mr. Shaw, baker ; Mr. Robert Philip, turner ; Mr. John Paton, wright ; Rev. David Black ; Mr. Andrew Scotland, manufacturer ; Mr. Robert Murray ; Dr. Thomson ; Dr. Hynd ; Dr. Farquharson ; Mr. John Moir ; Mr. James Alexander, manufacturer ; Mr. James Anderson, manufacturer ; Mr. John Cowie, merchant, High Street; Mr. Thomas Monteith, manufacturer (Mrs. Walker, post-office, and Mrs. Cargill's father), and his son Mr. William; Mr. James Henderson, manufacturer; Mr. John Henderson, manufacturer ; Mr. James Dagleish ; Mr. William Young ; Mr. Charles Murray ; Mr. Edward Meiklejohn ; Mr. James Galloway, sen. ; Mr. Andrew Thomson, builder ; Mr. Peter Paterson, builder; Mr. Robert Cairns, farmer; Mr. Blackney Waddell ; Mr. Lockhart Noble Cree, painter ; Mr. William Gillespie ; Mr. James Cairns; Mr. Alexander Johnston, the Alloa carrier; Mr. John Robertson. This long list brings forcibly home to the writer of these pages that he, too, must soon follow.

> ' A few more years shall roll,
> A few more seasons come,
> And we shall be with those that rest
> Asleep within the tomb.
>
> ' A few more suns shall set
> O'er these dark hills of time,
> And we shall be where suns are not,
> A far serener clime.
>
> ' A few more Sabbaths here
> Shall cheer us on our way ;
> And we shall reach the endless rest,
> The eternal Sabbath day.

    ' 'Tis but a little while,
      And He shall come again,
  Who died that we might live, who lives
    That we with Him may reign.
    ' Then, O my Lord, preprae
      My soul for that great day :
  O wash me in Thy precious blood,
    And take my sins away.'

CHAPTER XI.

TILLICOULTRY MADE INTO A BURGH.

WERE I to enter in detail into all the social, religious, and political movements and changes that have taken place in Tillicoultry since I came to it thirty-five years ago, it would fill another volume, and I must not therefore attempt the task. There is, however, one important event in connection with our local government, that took place in 1871, that I cannot but refer to, and that was getting our town and neighbourhood made into a burgh, with a staff of commissioners and chief magistrate to rule over us. The result has been that great improvements have been carried out, that cannot but have added greatly to the comfort of the inhabitants, and improved the health of the village; and notably amongst these are our beautifully paved footways and well-constructed run-channels along our streets, which have given our village quite a smart appearance, and put an end to those accumulations of stagnant water which used formerly to meet the eye everywhere. Even our 'Howdub' (Frederick Street), which used to be a regular puddle, and was most appropriately named, is now a smart, tidy-looking street, and quite as comfortable for those residing in it as any part of our village. Speaking of this street, I may, in passing, state that in 1805 it was the principal street of the

village, and formed part of the old highway from Dollar
to Stirling. At that time the new turnpike road was
not made along the foot of the Ochils ; and my old
friend Mr. Moir was telling me that he remembers well
of walking to Dollar on the old road, through Tillicoultry and Harviestoun estates, and *above* Broomrig,
Woodcot, and on by Gateside. It passed below Harviestoun Castle, about half-way between it and the present
road. It is now entirely shut up between Tillicoultry
and the villa of Belmont, near Dollar ; and also through
Mr. Johnstone's grounds, of Alva ; but it is still open
between Burnside of Alva and Menstrie.

The two-storied house at the west end of the ' Howdub,' Tillicoultry, was the principal inn of the village
in the days of the old road, and is one of the oldest
houses in it. It was latterly and for many years
conducted by a family of the name of Ure. A smaller
inn or public-house was in the same street ; and the
worthy proprietor of it had a very good motto on his
signboard, which it would be well for all business people
to adopt,—' Pay the day, and trust the morn ' (pay
to-day, and trust to-morrow). Of course, when to-
morrow came it was to-day ; and hence this prudent
man did business for ' ready money only.'

A good story is told of the proprietor of this
' public.' Smuggling was carried on very extensively
in James's day, and he had a pretty intimate acquaint-
anceship with all the smugglers of the district, and was
never at a loss for a plentiful supply of the genuine
' mountain dew ' when required, and very little of the
whisky consumed in his premises added much to the
king's revenue. Well, one day, when a neat little keg
that had recently been received was lying in a corner
of the kitchen, a neighbour came in to James, in great

P

haste, with the alarming news that the gauger was coming along the street, and would be in on him in a minute or two. What was to be done? The guidwife was out, and he could not, therefore, get her to help him in the emergency. The situation seeming desperate, there was nothing for it but to have recourse to a desperate expedient, and brave it out the best way he could. So, when the excise officer walked into the room, James was busy rocking the cradle, and crooning away some lullaby to the supposed infant that he—in the absence of his wife — was acting as nurse to. Apologizing to the Government official for not being able to leave the infant—the guidwife being out—he told him just to take a look through, and he would find things all in order. Being thrown off his guard by the apparent simplicity of the man, he satisfied himself with a cursory glance, and immediately left, to the no little relief, as we may suppose, of the worthy proprietor of the 'Pay the day and trust the morn' tavern. The keg was of course immediately removed from the cradle, and deposited in a safe place of keeping.

The proprietor of Tillicoultry estate at that time was lame, and James went frequently up to the big house, and assisted him in moving about ; and when he wished to have a survey of any part of the policies, where no conveyance could be made available, James carried him on his back. He was thus engaged one day, when, having said or done something that displeased the laird, he got his ears pulled for his trouble. This was too much for James's good nature ; so, spying a nice bank of nettles among some trees, he walked right into the heart of them, and, after giving him a good squeeze on one of the trees, dropped him down among the nettles, and went away and left him. We may be pretty sure James's services would not be required at the 'big house' after this, and that the laird would, during the rest of his days, have a wholesome dread of nettles.

Notwithstanding all the improvements that have been carried through (and they are many) since our Burgh Act was introduced, our assessment has never exceeded 1s. 1d. per £ on rental; and to those towns (such as Dollar) that are hesitating about adopting it, I would say, 'Don't delay another day.' (Archibald Walker, Esq., has been our chief magistrate in Tillicoultry ever since the Burgh Act was introduced, and no more worthy man could be got to fill the honourable position.)

The turnpike road was constructed in 1806 or 1807, and then commenced the building of the new part of all our villages along this road. Hence the name of 'the New Town' applied to that part of Dollar built on the new road.

CONSTRUCTION OF NEW CEMETERY IN TILLICOULTRY.

I will now only refer to one other important step that was taken by the inhabitants of Tillicoultry, in the year 1860, in resolving to construct a new cemetery on the south end of the Cunninghar Hill. It was completed in 1861, and the first interment that was made in it was that of our much-esteemed townsman, the late Dr. Ritchie. He had been residing in Glasgow for some time before his death; but when that event took place, his body was brought to Tillicoultry, and interred in our new cemetery on November 30th, 1861.

A handsome memorial-stone was erected to his memory, subscribed for by a great many of the inhabitants of the village, and other friends. The inscription on it is as follows :—

In memory of
DAVID S. RITCHIE,
who was the first interred
in this Cemetery, Nov. 30th, 1861.
Erected by
a large circle of friends
in admiration of his
Philanthropy and gratuitous
Professional Services
to the Poor.
' I was sick, and ye visited me.'

Under the thoroughly skilful management of Mr. Roberts, this cemetery has been beautifully laid out, and is quite an acquisition to our village, and a model of what the last resting-place of our friends ought to be. The suitability of the site fixed on, and the beauty of the situation, could not, I think, be surpassed anywhere.

The late Mr. Peter Dow took a great interest in the construction of our new cemetery, and it was his great ambition (as Inspector of Poor) to see it clear of debt before he died ; and in this he was gratified, as the last instalment was paid off just the year before his death.

THANKS.

And now, in conclusion, I beg to return my warmest thanks to all those who have kindly favoured me with information about events that happened before my time, and also for all information received of a more subsequent date, and trust I have presented it in such a form as will meet with their general approval.

APPENDIX TO THE FIRST EDITION.

HAVING, from the pressure of business and other causes, been unable to get my manuscript ready for the press till now, death in the meantime has been busy with some of those referred to in the foregoing pages. WARDLAW RAMSAY, Esq., of Whitehill and Tillicoultry, died in the month of July last, 1882 ; and his lady in about six weeks after. JAMES PATON, Esq., of Lethangie and Tillicoultry, died on the 9th of August 1882, aged eighty-five years. Mrs. Paton is left alone now in the old home ; and four members of his family, all married, and resident in different parts of the country, were left, along with her, to mourn his loss. Five of his family (three sons and two daughters) predeceased him. The first Mrs. Paton died on September 5th, 1850, aged forty-seven years. The first Mrs. David Paton (her sister) died 16th June 1853, aged forty-eight. ROBERT ARCHIBALD, Esq., of Devonvale, Tillicoultry, and Cluny Bank, Forres, their brother, died on the 24th September 1882, aged sixty-six ; Mrs. Gibson of Dollar (his sister) being the only one now left of the family. His widow and four sons were left along with her to mourn his loss. Two daughters predeceased him. Dr. TAIT (Archibald Campbell Tait), ARCHBISHOP OF CANTERBURY, who was born at Edinburgh in 1811, died at Addington Park, Croydon, on 3rd December 1882, aged seventy-one years, and was buried in Addington Churchyard on

December the 8th. His genealogy from 1682 is as follows:—William Tait, joiner in the village of Langside, Aberdeenshire, was the great-great-grandfather of the Archbishop. He died in 1739, aged fifty-seven years. His son Thomas—a mason at Thunderton— was father of John Tait, Writer to the Signet, Edinburgh, and of Harviestoun, Dollar, and Cumloden in Argyleshire; and John Tait's son Craufurd was the Archbishop's father.

DAVID MILLER, Esq., of Auchterarder, died last month after a short illness of only five days, aged eighty-three years, leaving his widow and three of a family to mourn his loss. When Mr. Miller and I paid a visit to Blackford churchyard in March last year, and laid bare part of the inscription on the old family tombstone,— that was of so much interest to us both,—we left instructions to have it all thoroughly cleaned and washed, so as to be able, if possible, to make out the whole of the inscription. On paying a subsequent visit to it, however, I was sorry to find that these operations had so rubbed away the letters as to make the first part of it almost unreadable, and the rest of it wholly so.

Having referred to the deep debt of gratitude Mr. Archibald of Beechwood had laid the town of Tillicoultry under, in building a handsome tower to our Town Hall, I have now to add that he has just supplemented his noble gift by ornamenting externally the Hall itself, at a cost of between £400 and £500, so as to be more in keeping with the beautiful tower; and now we have got such an elegant and commodious Town Hall as few country towns can boast of, and of which we have justly great reason to be proud.

W. G.

March 1883.

APPENDIX TO THE SECOND EDITION.

GREAT FLOOD IN 1883.

ON Thursday, the 2nd of August 1883, a similar flood to that of 1877 was again experienced on the south side of the Ochils. Between four and five o'clock in the afternoon, after a pouring-down rain, Tillicoultry Burn suddenly came down in one great wall of water of some seven or eight feet high, with a noise that was heard a great way off, and had a most alarming appearance. The suddenness of the rush, and the great volume of water, again made it evident that a waterspout or waterspouts had burst on the hills above us ; and it being only six years since a similar occurrence took place, and that previously no such event had happened during this century, the dwellers at the foot of the Ochils are beginning to feel justly alarmed at the frequency of such calamities, and to think that some great meteorological change is coming over the climate in this part of the country.

The damage done during this flood in Tillicoultry was comparatively trifling compared with the previous one, from the simple fact that we were better prepared for it. After that flood the burn was deepened, and strongly-cemented protecting walls built, and the water, till it reached Lower Mill Street, was confined to the channel of the burn. There, however, it again overflowed its bed, and the High Street was flooded for some hours to the depth of about three feet, and hundreds of tons of stones and gravel deposited on Lower Mill and High Streets. Four or five large streams of water were seen pouring over the tops of the hills, where usually no water runs. The general opinion seemed to be that the height of water in this flood was quite as great as that of 1877.

Dollar almost escaped the great rush of water this time, but in Alva there has been nothing seen like it during this century. The second uppermost stone bridge and retaining walls of the burn were swept away, while the lower houses of the Green Square were flooded to the depth of four feet. The water burst through the back wall of Mr. Perry's bakehouse, and, after completely wrecking it, rushed through Mr. Drysdale's shop, entirely destroying a large portion of his stock of books, paper, type, etc., causing serious loss to both gentlemen. Messrs. John Henderson & Son, manufacturers, and Mr. Porteous, also suffered considerable damage to their premises ; and a field to the east of their works was seriously flooded, and great loss sustained. This flood, *in Alva*, was very much more serious than that of 1877, the water having risen quite three feet higher. Great damage was done in the glen, and the dam-head filled to the brim with débris.

An Alva gentleman, who was driving over from Alloa, could not account for the singular appearance of the hills, as they seemed to be literally covered with white foam ; but when he got into Alva, and found a great part of the village deep under water, the mystery was then explained.

The 'Back Burn' at Tillicoultry House did enormous damage, a large portion of the garden wall having been thrown down, and a considerable piece of the garden completely wrecked. Mr. Cameron had his crops very seriously damaged, and his loss would come to a large sum. A deep gully of about a hundred yards in length and three to four feet wide was made in the road that passes his house, rendering it quite impassable. Mr. Orr's west lodge was again surrounded with water, and but for the loopholes which he had thoughtfully caused to be made in the wall at the south side of the public road after the last great flood, it would again probably have been tumbled over, as before, into the field.

CONTEMPLATED RAILWAY TO THE TOP OF BEN CLEUGH.

In these days of ocean telegraphs; great bridges over wide rivers—as at Queensferry and Dundee; proposed tunnels under broad arms of the ocean—as the Channel Tunnel to France; the gigantic ocean canals of the isthmuses of Suez and Panama; the Mont Cenis and St. Gothard tunnels; the talked of great canal of the Jordan Valley,—I don't think some of our go-ahead young folks would be very much surprised although they heard that it was proposed to have a tunnel through the centre of the globe, giving us a 'short cut' to Australia. Well, what is at present contemplated is *not quite* so alarming as that, but it is nothing less than a proposed railway to the top of Ben Cleugh. '*A railway to the top of Ben Cleugh!*' I think I hear some of our timorous ones say; 'why, it is enough to take away one's breath.' Yet so it is in verity, and the line has been actually surveyed, and it is seriously proposed, it is said, to carry the project through. Well, after that we really need not be surprised at anything. Good folks are

shaking their heads, and saying, 'Ah! it will never do.'
But have they good reason for saying so? Look at some
of the railways already constructed throughout the world
that are carried much higher than 2363 feet—the
height of Ben Cleugh. But then the cautious folks are
saying, 'Just think how it would disturb and annoy the
sheep.' Would it? I grant that for the first few days
it would; but after getting accustomed to the trains for
a week or two, they would not only not run away when
one was passing, but would actually scarcely condescend
to lift their heads to look at it. This we can see any
day in Glen Ogle, and other parts of the Callander and
Oban and on the Highland railways. I trust the scheme
will be carried through, as it will bring our beautiful
Ochils more into notice throughout the kingdom than
they have hitherto been, and attract crowds of tourists to
our really picturesque neighbourhood in the summer
season. The grand scenery on the Devon—at the
Caldron Linn, the Rumbling Bridge, the Devil's Mill,
the Black Linn of Glendevon, the Vicar's Bridge, etc.,
and the romantic old ruin of Castle Campbell, with the
really unsurpassed scenery of its beautiful glen, would
then become more widely known than they are at
present, great as is the number that annually visit them.
How delightful it would be, after visiting all the places
I have named, to finish up with a railway trip to the
top of Ben Cleugh, where the visitor would then behold
one of the finest panoramas, I believe, in the world.
That it is considered so by those who have travelled far
is the very general opinion. I have heard it told of a
gentleman, who once met the present worthy laird of
Alva (the proprietor of Ben Cleugh) when in the Holy
Land, that he remarked to him that in all his travels he
had nowhere beheld such magnificent scenery as from

the top of Ben Cleugh in Scotland ; and when he said so
he was ignorant of the fact that it *was* the laird of Ben
Cleugh he was talking to.

The most wonderful engineering feat that has yet
been accomplished—so far as *steep* railways are concerned—is the short line in Switzerland between
Montreux and Glion, which is the steepest railway in
the world. The ascent commences, and continues for
some little distance, at an angle of 32 degrees, which
then increases to 57 degrees. The carriages are raised
and lowered by means of a wire rope, and the various
patent breaks that are employed are considered so efficient, that, in the event of the rope breaking, the carriages
can at once be brought to a stand-still.

When the Edinburgh and Glasgow Railway was constructed, it was at that time considered essential to have
them as nearly level as possible ; and hence it is, I
understand, the most level railway in Scotland, and can,
in consequence, be wrought at less expense than any
other. To have thought then of making a railway to
the top of Ben Cleugh would have been considered sheer
madness. But now, with our increased experience, it
will be thought very little of.

THE MYSTERIOUS 'FOUNDLING' OF GATESIDE, DOLLAR.

I have now to record a most romantic story in real
life, connected with Gateside, around which a profound
mystery still hangs, and which probably may never be
thoroughly cleared up, but which is at this moment
engrossing the keen interest of a highly-respectable
family now resident in England. Exactly one hundred
and forty-one years ago, a beautifully-dressed baby boy

was found (by the then proprietor of the estate, Mr. Clerk Burns) lying in the malt-kiln of Gateside brewery; and enclosed in its dress a large sum of money, which clearly showed that this mysterious little stranger belonged to wealthy parents, whoever they were. All efforts to discover them, however, proving abortive, there was no alternative left but to adopt the little ' foundling,' which the good folks of Gateside accordingly did. Having made up their minds to do so, they then saw it to be their duty to have the child baptized; and following the custom—which at that time seems to have been generally adopted—of naming 'foundlings' after the place where they were found, he was baptized John Dollar, the first time, I believe, that the name of ' Dollar ' was ever applied to a family. (In connection with this giving of names to ' foundlings,' another case that happened about the same time in the neighbourhood of Dollar is very amusing. A baby girl was found at the head of a ' hairst-rigg,' and the good folks of Dollar had her baptized Jenny Rigghead.) I herewith give a copy of the registration of John Dollar's baptism, taken from the old session records of Dollar (now deposited in the Register Office, Edinburgh). It is as follows :—

' *Friday, July* 30*th*, 1742.

' Dollar. The child that was found in Clerk Burns' malt-kiln-logie was baptized.

' James Sorley, weaver in Dollar, being sponsor.'

This James Sorley would be Willie Sorley's grandfather, whom I used to hear very much spoken of in my young days, and who built the row of houses close to the crofts in the old town, and which then went (and, I suppose, still does) by the name of ' Sorley's Raw.'

After this mysterious ' foundling ' grew up to manhood, he suddenly and most unaccountably disappeared from Dollar, no one knew to where; and his exit from the locality created as much talk and surmise as his advent into it had done. It then seemed evident to all that during all those years he was in Dollar, the eye of her who had given him birth had been watching over him, and, when the suitable time came, had him removed from the locality, but where to was shrouded in mystery, and for a hundred and twenty years it has remained so. But now this mystery has so far been cleared up, and it is to be hoped that some day it will be all brought to light.

A stranger gentleman, Mr. Dollar, lately visited Dollar, and had come expressly from a southern county in England to make inquiries about an ancestor of his, whom he knew came from Dollar, but about whom he had little or no information, and was very anxious to learn something regarding him. His ancestor's name was peculiar, and a hundred and twenty years ago was unknown in England, till one day a gentleman suddenly and mysteriously made his appearance in the midst of the good folks of this southern county, but no one at the time knew from where, his name being John Dollar. Now, this John Dollar has numerous descendants in England, to the third and fourth generation, and it was one of those who came to Dollar a few weeks ago to make inquiry about this ancestor of his, who had, it seems, after he was settled in England for some time, made it known from what part of the world he had so mysteriously dropped in among them.

On hearing the story of the mysterious baby 'foundling,' Mr. Dollar became intensely interested, and in order to ascertain, if possible, the name of this infant, he went to Edinburgh, and searched the old session-records of Dollar, now deposited in the Register House. We can easily conceive, then, how immensely his interest would be increased when he discovered that this little foundling's name *was Dollar ;* and that now, therefore, part of the mystery that had rested over it for a hundred and twenty years was cleared away. He copied the entry from the session-records, a copy of which I have already given. It seems quite clear, then, that when the grown-up man John Dollar mysteriously disappeared from Dollar, he as mysteriously made his appearance in one of the southern counties of England, and that thus far, therefore, the mystery regarding him is cleared up. But *who* were his parents is still to be found out, and may be this may some day be accomplished.

There are parties living in Dollar at present who recollect well of their parents speaking of this ' foundling' baby of Gateside, and of the great excitement it caused in Dollar when it was discovered, and the very general desire that existed to find out who its parents were, but that this was never accomplished.

Here is a fine romance, then, in real life, and a splendid subject for some of our great romance writers of the present day, and perhaps some of them may be induced to take it up.

We can easily picture to ourselves the anguish of heart suffered by the poor mother of John Dollar, after leaving her helpless babe at Gateside on that to her most dreadful night, and what a terrible feeling of remorse would pursue her through all her after life.

A CORRECTION.

Since issuing the first edition of this book, I have learned from a gentleman who was a 'piecer' in his young days with old Mr. Paton, Kilncraigs, Alloa, when he commenced business, that stocking-yarn *was* spun there *before* the late Mr. John Mitchell came to Kilncraigs ; and that in the incident related by me in it in connection with this, Mr. Mitchell must have referred to some special new shade he had introduced, or some new description of yarn, and that I must have taken him up wrong. I now take this opportunity, therefore, of correcting the error, by omitting the paragraph altogether, and am very sorry the mistake had been made.

W. G.

TILLICOULTRY, *December* 1, 1883.